101 LIFE SKILLS FOR TEENS - THE ULTIMATE ADULTING HANDBOOK

HOW TO FIND A JOB, MANAGE MONEY, COOK & CLEAN, STAY SAFE ON THE ROAD & ONLINE, BUILD UNSTOPPABLE CONFIDENCE & SOCIAL SKILLS, & LIVE YOUR BEST LIFE

LIZ PANELLI

BLACKSTONE PUBLICATIONS

CONTENTS

Embarking on Your Journey   vii

PART I
Achieve Your Wildest Dreams: Mastering Soft Skills to Turn Vision into Reality   1

PART II
Navigating Your Emotions: Keys to Developing Resilience, Coping with Stress, and Finding Inner Peace   15

PART III
Healthy Habits, Happy Life: Holistic Health, Preventive Care, and Navigating the Medical System   25

PART IV
Smart Shopping for Smart Eating: Mastering the Art of Choosing Healthy Food While Saving Money   45

PART V
The Art of Cooking: Using Kitchen Appliances, Utensils, and Expert Techniques to Concoct Delicious and Creative Meals   57

PART VI
Clean Like a Pro: Keeping Your Home Clean, Fresh, and Inviting with Easy Cleaning and Laundry Hacks   83

PART VII
Home Sweet Home: How to Find and Maintain Your Perfect Living Space   99

PART VIII
On the Move: Mastering Skills for Safe and Confident Travel   113

PART IX
Money Matters Made Easy: Learning the Wealth-Building Blueprint for Lifelong Financial Fitness   131

PART X
Your Career Launchpad: A Comprehensive Guide
to Developing Professionalism in the Workplace   149

PART XI
Social Savvy: Unpacking the Unwritten Rules of
Social Interaction and Building Healthy Bonds   163

PART XII
Digital Defense: Mastering Essential Skills for
Keeping Yourself Safe in the Wild Wild Web   181

PART XIII
The Final Lesson: Things You Should Know That
We Can't Teach You   191

The Future is Yours   194

Notes   199
References   201

Copyright © 2023 by Blackstone Publications LLC

All rights reserved.

No part of this book may be reproduced, duplicated, or transmitted in any form or by any electronic or mechanical means, including information storage and retrieval systems, without written permission from the author or publisher.

Under no circumstances will any blame or legal responsibility be held against the publisher, or author, from any damages, reparation, or monetary loss due to the information contained within this book. Either indirectly or directly.

Legal Notice:

This book is copyright protected. This book is only for personal use. You cannot amend, use, distribute, sell, or quote any part of the content within this book without the consent of the author or publisher.

Disclaimer Notice:

Please note the information within this book is for educational and entertainment purposes only. All effort has been executed to present accurate, up-to-date, reliable, and complete information. No warranties of any kind are declared or implied. Readers acknowledge that the author isn't engaging in the rendering of legal, financial, medical, professional, or other health-related advice. The content within this book has been derived from various sources. Please consult a licensed professional before attempting any medical, financial, or health-related techniques or strategies outlined in this book.

By reading this document, the reader agrees that under no circumstances is the author responsible for any losses, direct or indirect, which are incurred as a result of the information contained within this document, including, but not limited to, errors, omissions, or inaccuracies.

EMBARKING ON YOUR JOURNEY

As a young adult, you are facing an ever-changing world filled with challenges that previous generations never had to face. Between the expectations of your parents, teachers, and friends, it can be hard to know what to do or where to turn. You may feel overwhelmed by the number of decisions you must face, the need to stay on top of your schoolwork and extracurricular activities, and the unknowns of what your future holds.

In addition to the challenges of the modern world, most young people aren't adequately taught skills for self-sufficiency in school settings - it's not part of the required curriculum to teach how to handle typical day-to-day tasks, such as running your own home, managing your finances, or succeeding in the workplace.

The impact of this skills and knowledge gap is profound: did you know that 1 in 4 adults in the United States feel that their debt is unmanageable,[1] 73% of adults don't follow a budget regularly,[2] over 75% feel stress daily,[3] and 68% of cars on the road aren't properly maintained for safety?[4]

Unfortunately, most teenagers feel just as unprepared for what adulting entails: nearly 1 in 5 university graduates don't know how to cook or do laundry,[5] 1 in 4 are lost with basic apartment maintenance,[5] over half of teens are worried about financing their futures,[6] and 80% of graduating university seniors have credit card debt before they even have a job. [7]

But what if there was a way that teens and young adults could gain confidence in their abilities to navigate these challenges? What if they could learn practical skills that would help them succeed not only in school but also in life beyond the classroom?

This is where this book comes in. In these pages, you'll find the guidance and support you need to thrive in the modern world – the skills that most people aren't taught and learn the hard way years later. You'll learn skills many adults struggle with for decades, wasting time, money, and energy. By mastering these skills well ahead of the norm, you will avoid the common pitfalls that are inescapable for most young adults entering the real world on their own for the first time.

But it's not just about avoiding mistakes – it's about achieving your dreams. With the tools and resources in this book, you'll be able to set and achieve goals, establish healthy habits, and create a life that you truly love. You'll be empowered to take charge of your future and become the best version of yourself.

Imagine a life where you're confident in your ability to care for yourself, both financially and emotionally. A life where you can create and maintain healthy relationships, romantic and platonic, opening you to a world of endless joy and authentic connection. Imagine having a strong sense of purpose and direction in life, where you can pursue your passions and build a career you love because you know how to bring your dreams into reality. This is the kind of life that you can create with decades of life knowledge condensed and summarized in this book.

Through easy-to-understand explanations and step-by-step instructions, you will gain the skills and confidence you need to thrive in the modern world independently. You'll learn the foundations for building lifelong success, creating fulfillment in your profession and relationships, sustaining exceptional physical and mental health, and much more. Whether you're getting ready to start your first job, are preparing to head off to college, or simply getting a jumpstart on what's to come in the exciting years ahead, this book will be your guide to creating the life of your dreams.

So if you're ready to take control of your life and become the best version of yourself, this book is for you. Let's get started on the path to your best life!

PART ONE
ACHIEVE YOUR WILDEST DREAMS: MASTERING SOFT SKILLS TO TURN VISION INTO REALITY

1. HOW TO IDENTIFY YOUR PURPOSE

WHAT IS 'PURPOSE'? Purpose is another word to describe one's larger vision, goals, and intentions for life. This is a question that humanity has asked themselves since some of the earliest thinkers and philosophers, like Aristotle and Socrates.[8]

Purpose doesn't have to be some big lofty goal like abolishing poverty, although this is a noble pursuit. A guiding purpose could be to travel the world and learn about other cultures, manage a business that impacts people's lives, make a difference in your community, create and nourish a loving family, or fight for a social cause like climate change.

To start, imagine you are 85 years old, sitting in a rocking chair, and looking back on your life. What would make you proud about your life? It could be a specific accomplishment, but it could also be how you lived your life (for example, through helping others, through kindness, and so on). What would you regret not having done or experienced?

Follow these steps to discover your purpose:

1. **Create an ideal life vision:** Before your purpose is to become clear, think about what a dream life looks like to you – how would you be living, how would you feel, what would your day look like, and who would you be surrounded by?

2. **Think about what evokes deep joy in you**: What lights in you that spark of excitement more than anything else? In what kinds of situations or doing what types of activities do you feel most connected to your heart, your sense of aliveness, or the people around you?

3. **Reflect on your interests, strengths, and values**: What matters most to you? What sorts of causes or injustices of the world speak to you most profoundly? What have people told you

you're great at? Doing what types of activities feel like minutes instead of hours to you?

4. **Try new experiences to discover new passions**: Broadening your horizons allows you to expand your identity beyond what you imagined for yourself, and it's in these surprising self-discoveries that you'll tap into your passion.

5. **Trust your instincts and follow your heart**: Learning to listen to your intuition will guide you to a life of fulfillment and authenticity, as you will pursue what makes you happy rather than satisfying others' desires or expectations.

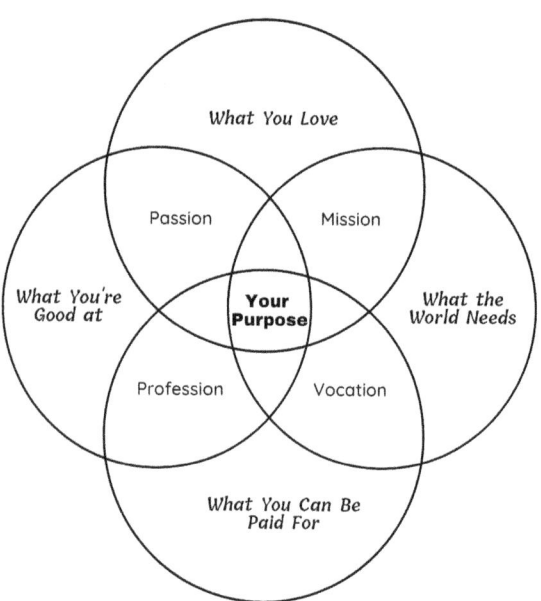

Remember that purpose can change and take many different forms over the course of our lives, so be gentle with yourself as you explore what feels right and re-align as you go.

2. HOW TO SET A S.M.A.R.T. GOAL

SETTING a S.M.A.R.T. goal is like crafting a roadmap to success - it provides a clear and specific direction towards reaching your desired outcome, just as a road map guides a traveler to their destination. Both help to define the journey and provide actionable steps to achieve the end result efficiently and effectively. Without setting a concrete goal, dreams are just a vision, but planning the process makes it real.

Let's break down what the acronym stands for:

1. **Specific:** Be clear and precise about what you want to achieve. The clearer your goal is, the easier it will be to create a plan of action. Ask yourself, "What exactly do I want to accomplish?" and "Why is this goal important to me?" Make the outcome as specific as you can.

2. **Measurable:** Make sure your goal can be quantified so that you can track your progress and determine whether you've achieved it. Ask yourself questions like "How much do I want to achieve?" and "How will I know when I've reached my goal?" Think about quantities, amounts, or percentages here.

3. **Achievable:** Set realistic goals that are within your reach with some stretch. While you should challenge yourself, you don't want to set yourself up for failure by creating an impossible standard. Ask yourself questions like "Is this goal within my abilities?" and "Do I have the resources I need to achieve this goal?"

4. **Relevant**: Make sure your goal is aligned with your values and long-term vision. Ask yourself, "Does this goal fit with my overall life plan?" and "Is this the right time to pursue this goal, or is there something I need to do first to ensure that I can be successful here?"

5. **Time-Bound:** Set a deadline for achieving your goal. This will give you a sense of urgency and help you stay focused. Other-

wise, it is much too easy to procrastinate. Ask yourself questions like "When do I want to achieve this goal?" and "What intermediate milestones can I set to help me stay on track?"

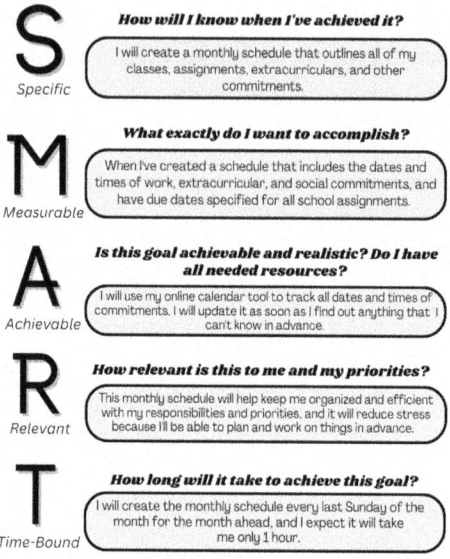

S.M.A.R.T. goals are powerful tools that can help you stay focused, motivated, and on track through the ups and downs of life. Master the SMART formula, and you will gain the clarity and direction you need to achieve your desired outcome and live a life that truly inspires you.

3. HOW TO PRIORITIZE

Prioritizing can seem overwhelming with so much on our plates in daily life - how to even go about choosing what we should and shouldn't do, let alone order and organize these tasks? Just as when packing for a trip, you need to carefully select which items to bring based on importance and limited space in the bag, you also need to prioritize tasks in order to achieve your goals. With the right tools and approach, this process can be manageable and even enjoyable:

1. **Write down everything you need to do**: From big projects to small tasks, make a list of everything you need to accomplish. This helps you get a clearer picture of what you need to prioritize.

2. **Evaluate each task's importance:** Consider the urgency and impact of each. Urgent tasks need to be done immediately, while important tasks have long-term consequences and should be prioritized accordingly.

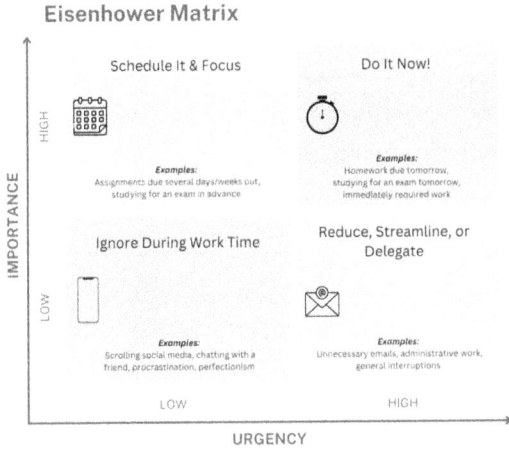

3. **Use the Eisenhower Matrix:** This strategy categorizes tasks into four categories: 1, Urgent and Important; 2, Important but Not Urgent; 3, Urgent but Not Important; and 4, Neither Urgent nor Important. Use the matrix to decide which tasks should be your top priority.

4. **Set deadlines for yourself:** Give yourself a timeline for each task so that you don't procrastinate. This will also help you stay

focused and motivated. Before starting, write down the amount of time you expect each task to take so that it becomes finite in your mind rather than some unachievable, impossible task.

5. **Minimize distractions:** Set aside time each day for focused work, and turn off distractions like notifications from your phone or computer.

6. **Take breaks:** Regular breaks can help you avoid burnout and increase productivity. Take a walk, stretch, or meditate for a few minutes to recharge your batteries.

7. **Review and adjust regularly**: Life is constantly changing, and so are your priorities. Review your list regularly and make adjustments as needed.

Remember, prioritizing is a process that takes time and practice. The more you do it, the easier it will become. Always be willing to adjust your priorities as needed to ensure you are putting your time and energy into what truly matters.

4. HOW TO MANAGE YOUR TIME

Time management can be challenging for many people, with school, extracurricular activities, socializing with friends, and family responsibilities all competing for our attention. But with a little organization and some smart strategies, you can get the most out of your time while still having fun:

1. **Create a schedule**: Write down all of your upcoming events, assignments, and responsibilities in a planner or calendar. This will help you stay organized and on top of things.

2. **Start your day with a plan:** Take a few minutes each morning to write down the most essential tasks you need to accomplish. This will give your day a sense of direction and keep you on track throughout the day.

3. **Use a timer:** Set a timer for specific tasks or blocks of time, such as 25 minutes of focused work followed by a 5-minute break. This will help you stay productive and keep your mind clear.

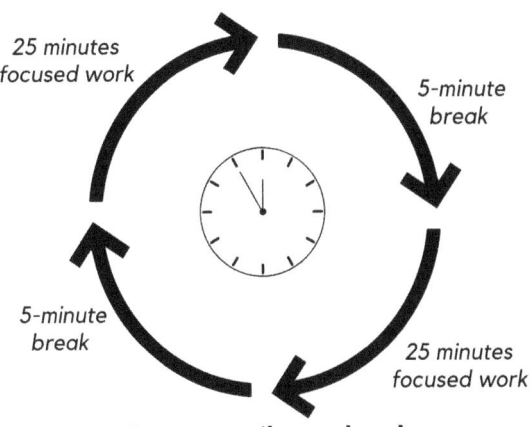

Repeat until completed
Take 10 minute breaks every hour

4. **Avoid distractions:** Distractions like social media, video games, or your phone can quickly consume your time. Have you ever gotten on your phone for what you told yourself would be ten minutes, but before you knew it, an hour had passed? Minimize distractions by turning your phone off and putting it away or setting strict limits on your screen time.

5. **Take breaks:** Taking ten-minute breaks every hour or so can help you stay refreshed, engaged, and focused. Use your breaks to stretch, eat a snack, or grab a breath of fresh air.

6. **Get enough sleep:** Sleep is essential for productivity and mental clarity. Make sure to get plenty of restful sleep each night so you can tackle the day ahead with energy and enthusiasm.

Remember, managing your time is about finding what works best for you. Experiment with different strategies and tools until you find a system that helps you stay organized and productive.

5. HOW TO MAKE A DECISION

Making a decision can be daunting, especially when faced with choices that will significantly impact your future, such as what career to pursue or whether to move to a new city. However, with strategic thinking and a clear sense of your priorities, you can feel confident making informed and thoughtful decisions that ultimately help you achieve your goals and create a fulfilling life:

1. **Identify the question and your priorities**: Before doing anything else, you must understand precisely what you are trying to decide - what is your ultimate goal in making this decision? Ask yourself, "What are my non-negotiables, and in what areas can I be more flexible?"

Take the typical scenario of choosing between universities: your ultimate aim may be to decide which university to attend out of all that you were accepted to. Suppose your priorities are that it must have your program of interest related to your desired career path, it must be within five hours of driving time from home, and you must have received some form of tuition assistance. You realize that you can be flexible with the size of the school if the other non-negotiable criteria are met.

2. **Gather information:** Once you clearly understand your priorities, educate yourself on all available options. Do your research and talk to people who have relevant experiences or knowledge if needed. Make sure you look for relevant, credible, and unbiased information. Consider different perspectives, expert opin-

ions, and personal experiences; however, remember that you do not need to give any individual's opinion extra weight – simply take it as evidence to consider alongside everything else you gather.

3. **Consider the pros and cons:** List each option's positive and negative aspects. Compare them side-by-side, and get a sense of whether the option is more heavily weighted towards positives or negatives concerning your priorities and overarching goal. Compare this across all of your options.

4. **Trust your instincts:** Sometimes, no matter how much information you gather or how much logic and rationality you use, you just have a gut feeling about what is right. Pay attention to your intuition, as it is an invaluable decision-making tool. Use your gut feeling in combination with your logical analysis, and assess whether there's an option that jumps out.

5. **Don't overthink it:** Don't let fear or anxiety hold you back. Making decisions can feel scary, but more often than not, the best decision is the one that feels right. Trust yourself and take action.

Making decisions is a natural part of life. It's okay to make a choice that doesn't work out - there's no such thing as failure as long as you learn from it and keep moving forward.

6. HOW TO BUILD A ROUTINE

A daily routine is similar to a well-oiled machine: just as all parts of a machine function automatically and seamlessly together to accomplish a complicated task, a daily routine takes the thought and analysis paralysis out of structuring your day, thereby making your daily functioning more efficient and consistent over the long-term.

Have you ever told yourself you would work out or study, but you never made time to do it because you didn't schedule it into your day? Building a routine ensures that the things important to you get done because you make time for them in advance. Here are some ideas to get you started in creating your own daily, weekly, or monthly routine:

1. **Make a to-do list:** Start each day by writing down the top activities and tasks you want to make sure you prioritize every day. This could include exercise, studying, or cooking a healthy meal.

2. **Establish a routine schedule:** Decide the best times for each activity and block out time in your schedule accordingly. For example, do you have time for physical activity in the morning, afternoon, or evening? Remember to be realistic and leave space for unexpected events or tasks that may arise.

3. **Review your routine each day:** Take a few minutes each morning to review what you have scheduled for the day. For example, perhaps Wednesdays are your math class study day, while Thursdays are your days to take your sister to the park.

4. **Stick to a schedule:** Adhere to your routine as much as possible, even on weekends. It can be easy to make excuses to not do the things that are important to us, but come back to your reasons for making the routine in the first place – committing to yourself to work on your goals so that you actually achieve them. Consistency is key, not perfection!

5. **Be flexible:** While sticking to your routine is important, feel free to adjust it if it's not working for you. Life is unpredictable, so be flexible and adapt your routine as needed. But be honest with yourself about why you're adjusting your routine – is it because you're finding it too draining or because it's pushing you outside of your comfort zone? Growth is uncomfortable but necessary to succeed in life.

6. **Have fun with it:** Building a daily routine doesn't have to be strict or dry. Get creative and find ways to make your routine fun and enjoyable. This will make it easier to stick to and help you feel more fulfilled and motivated while working towards what's important to you.

PART TWO
NAVIGATING YOUR EMOTIONS: KEYS TO DEVELOPING RESILIENCE, COPING WITH STRESS, AND FINDING INNER PEACE

7. HOW TO REGULATE YOUR EMOTIONS

EMOTIONS ARE part of the human experience – they are the 'flavors' of life. From joy to sadness to excitement, disgust, and anger, feeling emotions is normal and healthy. Through emotional regulation techniques, we can get a grip on our emotions so that they don't cause us to do and say things that aren't in tune with the person we want to be.

When you notice an emotion coming up, ask yourself, "Do I want to deal with this emotion healthily, do I want to ignore it, or do I want to react to it?" Experiment with these strategies the next time you feel intense emotions coming to the surface:

1. **Try 'bubble breathing':** Use the 4-6-7 rule for deep breathing. Inhale through your nose for 4 seconds, hold for 6 seconds, and exhale through your mouth for 7 seconds. Repeat as many times as you need.

2. **Use progressive muscle relaxation:** Ground into your body, tense, and then release different muscle groups. Start by naming your emotions, then visualize them in various muscle groups while you actively tense those muscles. Hold for 5 seconds, then release. Repeat with other muscle groups – wrist and fingers,

shoulders, knees and thighs, feet and toes, and neck. This releases palpable tension from your body where you may be holding it.

3. **Keep a fidget toy on hand:** Pull it out to release what you're feeling: In moments of stress, visualize your emotions in your body, then release them into the fidget toy. As you pull back and forth or spin the object, feel your emotions being released from your body with every movement. Use with any other similar object.

4. **Talk to yourself like a best friend:** Tell yourself 10 things you genuinely like about yourself. Then give yourself a pep talk and hype yourself up as you would a close friend.

5. **Shake your body out:** Go on a walk, run, dance, play any sport, or engage in physical activity. Do anything to shake up your body and release pent-up energy.

6. **Scream into a pillow:** No one has to hear it, and you can get excess emotional energy out of your body when pent up. Give it a try, and see how much better you feel afterward.

---

8. HOW TO DEAL WITH FEELINGS OF STRESS OR OVERWHELM

With all the various things young people have to balance in their daily lives, from juggling school pressures to part-time work to maintaining relationships with peer groups, exploring dating, and engaging in extracurriculars, it is no wonder that 64% of teens report feeling stressed.[9]

Whenever you feel trapped in emotions of stress or overwhelm, try the following strategies to noticeably ease the tension:

1. **Breathe deeply:** Recognize that you are not your emotion. Knowing that you are separate from an intense feeling in the

middle of experiencing it is a significant breakthrough to be celebrated. Next time you feel like you are losing control, focus on one thing only – taking deep breaths.

2. **Accept your feelings:** Avoid judging yourself for your emotions. Remember that you are a typical human being experiencing typical human emotions. There is nothing inherently bad or wrong about the feelings that you experience.

3. **Reframe:** Try looking at the situation from another perspective. There is always a silver lining to be found. For example, feeling frustrated or overwhelmed signals that we're about to have a breakthrough in learning something new. Feeling these emotions can be quite positive because it means we are challenging ourselves to grow.

4. **Focus on what you can control:** Our brains have the superpower of hyper-focusing on negativity and perceived threats to keep us safe. But this can often cause more harm than good, especially when it leaves us feeling hopeless and disempowered. Instead of fixating on what's going wrong, focus on what you can do right now. And remember, it's almost always more than you may think.

5. **Take a break:** If you're still feeling overwhelmed, it's perfectly okay to take a break and return when ready. The important thing is to set an intention before leaving the task so that procrastination doesn't take over instead. For example, say to yourself, "I will take a 10-minute walk around the block to settle this frustration, and then I'll come back to finish my homework."

---

9. HOW TO DEVELOP A SELF-CARE PLAN

Self-care can be compared to refueling a car. Just as a car needs fuel to run, our bodies and minds need self-care to function at their best. Just like you wouldn't drive a car on empty, it's important to take care of ourselves to avoid burnout.

There are six parts to the 'self-care wheel' that keep the whole car moving smoothly and in control. When developing a self-care plan, be sure to touch on the following areas:

1. **Physical (care for the body):** This includes getting enough sleep and proper nutrition, engaging in exercise like jogging, yoga, or swimming, staying hydrated, and avoiding inflammatory foods like sugars.

2. **Social (relationships with others):** Spend time with loved ones, join clubs or groups, join a faith-based community, or volunteer for a cause you're passionate about – we humans are social creatures, and connection is an absolute must.

3. **Emotional (healthy processing and expression of emotions):** Express yourself creatively - whether through writing, drawing, painting, or playing music – creative expression is a healthy way to process what's inside. Use meditation or yoga for stress relief and deep breathing, and do activities that bring you joy.

4. **Occupational (school and work):** Maintaining your responsibilities at school and work is important to support yourself and live with pride and fulfillment. Deep down, it doesn't feel

good for most people to drop their obligations. At the same time, maintaining balance is essential. Remember to set achievable goals, take breaks, and be proud of your accomplishments.

5. **Spiritual (core values, meaning, and purpose):** Spiritual self-care is all about connecting deeply to yourself and the world around you, practicing gratitude, recognizing abundance in your life, and finding meaning in whatever you're doing.

6. **Rejuvenation (rest and replenishment):** Intentional rest allows your body and energy to reset. Play gives you that joyful zest and passion for life, a spark you can carry into your daily activities. It's essential to carve some time out here to fuel you up for everything you wish to create in life.

Learn to check in with yourself weekly or even daily on these six parts of the wheel – if one area feels depleted, focus on extra self-care while maintaining the others with at least one small action a day.

---

10. HOW NOT TO COMPARE YOURSELF TO OTHERS

All of us have compared ourselves to others at some point in our lives. With the rise of social media, these constant comparisons are even more prevalent. Basing our self-worth on our perceptions of others is a recipe for unhappiness, doubt, and despair. Thankfully, there are proven strategies for mitigating these harmful effects of comparison, and the best part is that this is all in the power of our minds!

1. **Observe the behavior:** Change happens when we notice what we're doing. The next time you feel negatively about yourself, dig a bit deeper. What triggered you to go down this thought path? Were you on social media, were you watching a reality TV

show, or were you comparing your grades to those of your friends?

2. **Redirect your thoughts:** One powerful way of doing this is by putting the focus back onto yourself in a positive way. Use the 3x3 rule: think of 3 things you like about yourself, 3 things you're proud of that you've accomplished, and 3 things you're grateful for.

When stuck in comparison...

3 What are 3 things I like about myself?

3 What are 3 things I'm proud of?

3 What are 3 things I'm grateful for?

Show Yourself Kindness

3. **Remind yourself that nobody is perfect:** The image that people portray is just what they want others to see. What people show online is almost always the tip of the iceberg of all of the emotions, insecurities, and doubts they face daily. The next time you feel jealous, not good enough, or down on yourself because you are looking at someone else's highlight, remember that they are also a human, feeling many of the same things you are.

4. **Only compare to yourself:** Comparing ourselves to others does nothing but make us feel bad. It's destructive. Instead, compare yourself to yourself – have you grown in skill, ability, or

knowledge in the past month or several months? If so, celebrate that. Have you taken steps out of your comfort zone in the past year? Celebrate that! Use self-comparison in a healthy way to ensure you make consistent strides to keep growing and learning.

11. HOW TO PRACTICE MINDFULNESS

"In today's rush, we all think too much, seek too much, want too much, and forget about the joy of just being." – Eckhart Tolle

Engaging in a simple daily mindfulness practice of just 5-10 minutes can have massive positive changes in your perceptions of and relation to your inner world. Do any of these exercises as a preventive measure or in response to a strong emotional state that arises. Make the commitment to implement at least one of the following techniques every day:

1. **Body awareness:** Check in with your body. Where are there aches, pains, or tingles? Where are there good sensations? Where is there no sensation? What else can you feel?

2. **Heart awareness:** Bring your focus to your heart. What sensations can you feel? Is it heavy or light? If you could give it a color, what would it be? Would it be bright or dull? Now imagine breathing in gold light and having that light fill up your heart and clear away any and all pain.

3. **5-4-3-2-1 exercise:** This technique gets your focus out of your head and into the environment around you: what are 5 things you can see right now? Observe every detail about them. What are 4 things you can touch? Be observant of their different textures. What are 3 things you can hear? Feel the sound waves

in your ears. What are 2 things you can smell? Smell the multi-faceted aroma. What's 1 thing you can taste?

4. **Breath focus:** Where do I feel the sensations in my body when I breathe in and when I breathe out? How deep are my breaths? What is their natural speed without my involvement or focus?

5. **Gentle observation of thought:** Imagine sitting on a river and watching the flow of thoughts rush by in the water while you sit on a rock. How fast are your thoughts moving? How loud are they? What energy are they conveying?

6. **Active listening:** Tune into others' communication as deeply as you can. What is this person communicating beyond their words? What is their body language saying? What kind of words are they using, and is there any clear sense of why that may be?

Daily mindfulness practice is like giving your brain a spa day - it provides a moment of peace and rejuvenation from the hustle and bustle of daily life, allowing you to return to your tasks with a clear and focused mind, ready to tackle whatever stressors or surprises comes your way.

PART THREE
HEALTHY HABITS, HAPPY LIFE: HOLISTIC HEALTH, PREVENTIVE CARE, AND NAVIGATING THE MEDICAL SYSTEM

12. HOW TO ACHIEVE 100-YEAR HEALTH: THE 6 PILLARS OF HEALTH & WELL-BEING

THERE IS SO much to experience in a lifetime, and you are just getting started. Living to 100 years old is no longer an anomaly – the oldest person currently living is 115 years old![10] To ensure that you have as many years as possible on this earth to live your dreams, create and nurture a family (in whatever form that takes), and enjoy the simple pleasures of being a human, all while in pain-free health that allows you to move how you want when you want, it's essential to integrate these 6 scientifically proven principles into your lifestyle.

PILLAR 1: FUEL YOUR BODY WITH PROPER NUTRITION

The food put into our bodies leaves an impact far beyond what can be seen with the eye. The micro and macronutrients that food is made of provide instructions that dictate how the body functions in the present and the future – if it is given the wrong instructions, over time, the body will express this disconnect through chronic ailments like arthritis, gastrointestinal issues, diabetes, heart problems, and even autoimmune disease.[11] In the short term, we feel fatigued, brain fogged, low energy, and depleted.

When we provide our bodies with the fuel that they truly need, in the right qualities and quantities, we not only feel mentally better in the moment, but we are much less likely to develop chronic disease in the medium to long term that will drain LOTS of money, time, and happiness from our quality of life. Why not prevent all of this if it's entirely within our power?

Foods with added sugars, like sweets and sugary desserts, processed foods like white bread or processed meat (think hot dogs, bologna, and deli meats), and deep-fried foods like French fries should be avoided entirely. Beyond their immediate impacts on lowering your energy, foods like these trigger inflammation in the body, particularly the gut.[12]

Recent studies have unearthed the massive link between gut health and mental health: up to 90% of the body's serotonin, a neurotransmitter known to regulate mood and social behavior, is produced in the gut, and disruptions to the gut microbiome, such as through an imbalance of good and bad bacteria, have been linked to various mental health conditions such as depression and anxiety.[13]

Next time you eat something you know isn't good for your body, pay attention to how you feel mentally afterward, and compare this to how you feel after something healthy – let this difference be motivation to cut these foods out!

PILLAR 2: ENGAGE IN REGULAR EXERCISE

It's no secret that exercise is an essential key to warding off disease and staying healthy, but scientific evidence also shows that consistent physical activity helps you live longer.[14] Not only does it reduce the likelihood of death from preventable diseases like heart disease, obesity, or diabetes, but exercise also causes cellular changes that keep the body younger and living longer.[15]

One study showed a 9-year difference in the aging of cells between a physically active person and someone who was not![15]

Integrating consistent physical activity into your life has massive health benefits. For example, people who walk briskly for just 20 minutes a day live, on average, 7 years longer than those who don't! Why exactly is this? Exercise has an anti-inflammatory effect, the key to disease prevention, and improves immune and digestive system functioning.[15]

Exercise's impact on mental health and cognitive functioning is similarly shocking: scientific research shows that exercise can treat mild to moderate depression just as well as antidepressant medication – without side effects![16] This is due to many complex and interacting pieces – exercise promotes all sorts of changes in the brain, such as neural growth that promotes feelings of peace and well-being. It also releases endorphins, powerful chemicals in your brain that energize your spirits and lift your mood. On top of that, exercise serves as a distraction and redirect of focus, allowing for breaking the cycle of negative thoughts that feed depression.[16]

Regular physical activity can reduce anxiety and stress by providing an outlet for relieving tension and releasing emotional energy in the mind and body. It can help diminish symptoms of ADHD by improving concentration, motivation, memory, and mood while boosting the brain's dopamine, norepinephrine, and serotonin levels—all of which affect focus and attention.[16]

So, given all these massive benefits, what's one reason you'll commit to engaging in at least 20 minutes of physical activity daily? Keep coming back to that reason, and let it spark your drive!

PILLAR 3: GET ENOUGH SLEEP

Getting enough sleep each night has all sorts of overlooked health benefits.[17] It can help with the following:

- Reducing stress and improving mood
- Thinking more clearly
- Performing better at school and work
- Getting along better with people
- Getting sick less often
- Making good decisions and avoiding accidental injuries
- Staying at a healthy weight
- Avoiding chronic illnesses like diabetes and heart disease

It may be shocking to hear what a profound effect getting enough sleep has on your mental health and brain functioning, but it's true – sleep deprivation can worsen symptoms of anxiety and depression, which then, in turn, make sleep more difficult.[17] It's a vicious cycle that worsens over time and can lead to serious mental health outcomes. If you've been feeling low moods lately, check in with yourself on how much sleep you've been getting and how restful it has been.

So how much sleep should you really be getting? Teenagers need more rest than the 7 hours required for most adults. Their brains and bodies are undergoing radical changes; therefore, they need an additional 1-3 hours per night (8-10 hours total) for energy replenishment and rejuvenation.[18] It's also essential to stay on the same sleep schedule as often as you can, as this trains your body's biological clock and circadian rhythm to fall asleep faster, enter a deep state of sleep more quickly, and stay there longer - all so that you wake up feeling even more refreshed and with the mental clarity and energy to tackle your day!

PILLAR 4: AVOID TOXINS

Alcohol and nicotine are so readily accessible that their use is quite normalized. But there's no denying these substances for what they are – poisons. Smoking and drinking alcohol have long been known to increase the likelihood of many devastating chronic illnesses manifesting in the body, such as heart disease, diabetes, and even 7 types of cancers![19] Both smoking and drinking are linked to inflammatory bowel disease, nerve pain, liver failure, and loss of blood flow to the brain. They even contribute to mental and cognitive disorders like dementia by shrinking brain size.[20]

You may be wondering if vaping is a healthier way to consume nicotine since it eliminates the carcinogens and poisons that are well-known to be included in cigarettes. The answer is no, as vaping has some severe health consequences. The aerosol fumes contain ultrafine particles that are inhaled deep into the lungs, with chemicals in the flavorings linked to lung disease. They also have dangerous compounds like those found in car exhaust, and heavy metals like nickel, tin, and lead.[21] None of that is meant to be put in the human body.

New research has also shown that vaping and nicotine worsen symptoms of depression and anxiety - people who vape have twice the chance of having a diagnosis of depression![22] Nicotine is also found to be more correlated with (or have a higher chance of occurring in) people who have ADHD symptoms.

If you vape or smoke, you may not have even realized how it's damaging your mental health, and over time, this can have serious impacts on your physical health as well! Why make it harder for your brain to support a positive mood if it's entirely within your control?

PILLAR 5: CREATE HEALTHY SOCIAL CONNECTIONS

Most of us have heard how important nutrition, sleep, and physical activity are on health, but did you know that social connections have just the same level of impact? One recent research study even showed that low social connectedness has an even stronger negative effect on one's health than high blood pressure, obesity, or even smoking![23]

Having strong social connections in your life:

- Strengthens your immune system and ability to fight off illness
- Helps you recover from disease faster
- Lowers levels of anxiety and depression
- Increases self-esteem
- And even leads to a 50% increased chance of longevity[24]

Conversely, not having fulfilling social connections in one's life can lead to depression, poor sleep quality, impaired cognitive and executive function (i.e., ability to do our day-to-day tasks), accelerated and worsening brain decline, susceptibility to illness, and even earlier death.[25]

The interesting part about all of this is that the level of social connection you feel is subjective – meaning that you don't need to have a set number of friends to have these health benefits. There's no measurement of how 'strong' a relationship needs to be to have a protective effect. Instead, it's all about how YOU feel about the relationship, how fulfilling it feels to you, and how much value it adds to your life from your perspective.

PILLAR 6: DEVELOP A PRACTICE OF MINDFULNESS

Over 61% of teens today feel pressure to perform highly academically, and at least a third feel pressure to look or act a certain way socially.[26] If this overwhelming pressure and stress remain stuck in the body, they can lead to many diseases and ailments.[27]

So how can stress be managed and reduced? Mindfulness is all the hype these days, but it's not without good reason. Mindfulness has many physical and mental health benefits that are too significant to ignore, including stress management.

Here are some notable benefits of mindfulness:[28]

- Gives you greater control over your reactions and impulses
- Improves your working memory, so that you perform better at work and at school
- Strengthens your ability to focus and eliminate distracted thoughts
- Reduces symptoms of depression and anxiety by lowering stress and rumination (being stuck and looping on a thought)

Mindfulness doesn't have to be a formal practice where you sit on the ground with your eyes closed, although it's that too. Remember that it can be as simple as being present in your day-to-day - purposefully noticing the smells, textures, sounds, and sights around you. Make a simple vow to yourself to tune in to your internal experience and to not be ruled by the thoughts and emotions that come and go that are simply part of the human experience.

How will you integrate at least a few minutes of mindfulness into your routine each day?

How will you practice each of the pillars each day?

13. HOW TO CHOOSE A DOCTOR

Choosing a doctor is not something to take lightly. To receive the best care possible, whether through ongoing, routine visits to a primary care physician or in the specialized treatment of a specific issue, doing your due diligence will ensure you get the best, most tailored care for YOU.

1. **Check their credentials and length of practice:** You can also look for reviews and ratings online, but it's an added bonus if you can find a doctor recommended by someone you know.

Having trust in a doctor's skill and experience fit to your situation is essential.

2. Think about what you need to feel comfortable and psychologically safe: Medical appointments can be pretty vulnerable, whether physically in the examination or solely in the personal information shared, which is why it's essential that you feel seen, understood, and respected.

3. **Take your time to decide:** If you aren't sure whether a particular doctor or practice will be a good fit, you can always attend one consultative appointment and decide whether you'd like to return. Never feel pressure to continue care if anything feels off.

Above all, finding a doctor you can connect with and chat openly with is critical for top-notch care. Trust and comfort make all the difference!

Experience   Expertise   Connection   Comfort   Communication

14. HOW TO SCHEDULE A MEDICAL APPOINTMENT

Once you've chosen your doctor based on what's important to you, you're ready to schedule an appointment.

There are several ways to schedule an appointment, most commonly by phone or online. If you have questions you'd like to ask before scheduling, such as about payment or the expected length of the appointment, it's better to schedule by phone to get answers right away.

You'll need to know the following when scheduling an appointment, whether by phone or online:

1. **Your availability:** Are you only free at a particular time of day? Or are you open at any time on a specific day?

2. **Your insurance information:** This varies by country of residence, but the receptionist will use this information to let you know how much payment will be.

3. **What issue is bringing you to seek care:** You can be as specific or general as you like when scheduling, but they need to know the general issue to understand how much time to allocate to your visit and how to inform the doctor. For example, you could say that you are seeking to schedule a primary care check-up, an assessment about chronic migraines, or to get a mole checked out.

When you visit a doctor's office for the first time, there will always be some basic paperwork to complete. This is so that the doctor can get to know you better ahead of time so that they can ultimately treat you more effectively.

Typically, you will need to be able to provide:

1. Your allergies
2. Any history of chronic illness, hospitalizations, or surgeries
3. Your current medications: names, dosages, and how frequently per day you take them
4. A description of the symptoms that bring you into the office, and your frequency of experiencing them

15. HOW TO ADVOCATE FOR YOURSELF IN A MEDICAL APPOINTMENT

Speaking up around authority figures can feel scary, especially if you've ever had an experience where you weren't listened to. This is why learning to advocate for yourself, in and outside the doctor's office, is so important.

Self-advocacy means that you are armed with the necessary tools to stand up for yourself, whether with specific information, language, or confidence. In the medical care space, this means that you can be direct about what you believe you need in terms of your health and that you have a right to discuss or refuse certain treatment options.

What you can do to increase your self-advocacy skills:

1. **Prepare before the appointment:** Make notes of everything you're experiencing out of the ordinary, including any new symptoms, and be sure to bring it with you, so you don't forget anything.

2. **Commit to communicating what's on your mind:** Clinicians can only know what we tell them. All the more detail you can give them just means the more they can make better judgments.

3. **Take notes during the appointment:** Sometimes, so much information is provided that leaving and not remembering everything said is possible. Taking notes isn't weird, and you'll leave feeling in control of what to do next.

4. **Ask lots of questions:** Especially if you don't understand anything about what was communicated. Some doctors are in a rush, and some aren't good with people skills, so you shouldn't hesitate to speak up with an "Um, hold up, can you explain what exactly that means?"

5. **Remember that you are in control:** Only you hold the power to decide which next steps are right for you.

ESSENTIAL SCRIPTS TO PRACTICE:

- "I'm not sure what you mean by [X]; could you explain that further?"

- "Can you elaborate more on what that route of [treatment, medication, etc.] entails?"
- "What are the side effects? Should I be concerned about them?"
- "I know what I'm experiencing, and it's [X, Y, Z]."
- "No, that's not the right option for me. I'd rather do [X, Y, or Z]."

16. HOW TO REFILL A PRESCRIPTION

If you need to take a medication that has been prescribed by a medical professional, whether for a short-term malady like an infection or for a chronic, long-term illness, you will need to know how to get your prescription refilled on time so that you never leave your health on rocky ground.

Prescriptions are typically filled once every month – meaning the bottle of medicine that you receive lasts only about 30 days. So when your medicine supply is running low, usually around when you only have a week's worth remaining, you should call the pharmacy.

You should always leave prescribed meds in their original container. On the bottle, you'll have all of the information that you'll need:

1. The number of refills remaining
2. Pharmacy phone number
3. Prescription number
4. Instructions on:

- **What the medication looks like**: it's important to check that you weren't given the wrong medication, especially when starting a new one. It's also helpful information for security personnel when traveling via plane with your meds.

- **How to take the medication:** including what time of day, what dosage, how frequently, and any other special instructions like whether to take it with food.

When you pick up your prescription from the pharmacy, if you ever have any questions, remember that you can always ask the pharmacist anything you may be unsure about so that you can confidently know that you're taking the medication correctly and safely.

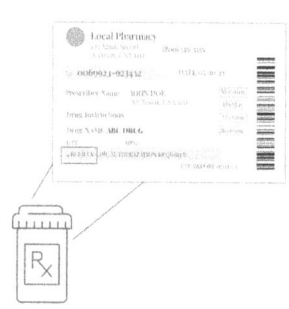

17. HOW TO CORRECTLY USE OVER-THE-COUNTER MEDICATIONS

Over-the-counter (OTC) medications are any medicines you don't need a prescription to buy and can pick up in your local drug store, such as cold or flu, allergy, or pain reliever medicines.

Even though OTC medications don't require a prescription, they are still products that impact the body. Studies estimate that approximately 10,000 emergency room visits by children and teens under 18 each year are due to incorrect use of OTC medications.[29] Therefore, even seemingly harmless medications must be used with caution and understanding.

Remember these best practices when using OTC medicines:

1. **Read and follow the label every time you take medication**: Look for things like how much to take based on your weight and

age and how frequently to take it. Never take medicine in a shorter period than what's listed on the label.

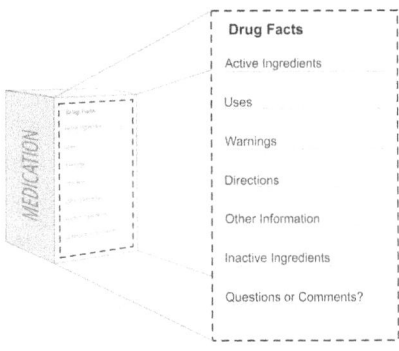

2. **Only take medications with one active ingredient at a time:** don't mix anything without speaking to a pharmacist first to ensure the combinations are safe. For example, ibuprofen and acetaminophen are pain relievers but have different chemical make-ups: Aleve is made from ibuprofen, while Tylenol uses acetaminophen. If you have a headache, you shouldn't take both as you'd be mixing ingredients. Stick to one; mixing can cause overdoses.

3. **Never mix acetaminophen and alcohol:** Ingesting both within the same time window can cause serious liver damage.[30]

4. **Take any medicines with the guidance of a parent or doctor:** Whenever in doubt, don't guess. It could cause more harm than good. Always check with a parent or doctor if you have concerns or questions.

18. HOW TO RECOGNIZE AND TREAT A COLD VERSUS A FLU

You can't sleep because you wake up from coughing, can't breathe from a stuffed nose, or because your muscles hurt...I'm sure you've experienced this before. But is it a cold or the flu?

It can sometimes be tricky to tell, especially when the symptoms first come on strong. Colds and the flu are contagious respiratory illnesses caused by viruses that spread through contact with another person through coughing, sneezing, or touching infected surfaces. Colds generally do not cause serious or lasting health problems, while flu cases can get dangerous enough to cause lasting damage if not treated properly.

Knowing the difference between a cold and the flu is vital to getting better quickly. So how can you tell?

Here's a simple shortcut that works more often than not: [31]

1. Are my main symptoms of sneezing and a runny nose? If so, it's most likely a cold.

2. Do I have a fever? Am I fatigued? Do I have body aches or chills? If yes, it's most likely the flu.

Remember, the signs above are usual but not set in stone, so it's always a good idea to talk to a doctor for a proper diagnosis and treatment plan, especially if you are experiencing severe or worsening symptoms.

---

19. HOW TO PERFORM BASIC FIRST AID

Imagine this scenario: Your friend is playing basketball and takes a nasty fall; suddenly, you are the only one there to help. Would you know what to do? Knowing basic first aid can give you the confidence and ability to assist someone in need and potentially save a life. Here's how to perform basic first aid in 4 simple steps:

1. **Remain calm:** If someone is in a predicament, it's important to keep a level head and remain focused. By doing so, you will be able to think more clearly and bring a sense of calm to the injured or unwell individual.

2. **Evaluate the emergency:** Take a moment to assess the situation and determine what first aid measures are required. Check for any obvious signs of serious injury or illness, such as heavy bleeding, struggling to breathe, or loss of consciousness.

3. **Call for help:** If it's a serious emergency, call your local emergency services. Clearly explain the situation and location, and stay on the line until you receive further instructions.

Signs of Alcohol Poisoning...

 **P**UKING WHILE PASSED OUT

 **U**NRESPONSIVE TO PINCHING OR SHAKING

 **B**REATHING IS SHALLOW OR HAS STOPPED

 SKIN IS BLUE, COLD, OR CLAMMY

Remember the acronym PUBS
If even one of these is true, call emergency services immediately

4. **Stop bleeding:** If the person is bleeding, apply direct pressure to the wound with a clean cloth or tissue. Keep pressure on the wound until the bleeding stops or emergency services arrive.

5. **Comfort the injured person:** Keep the person calm and still, and keep them warm. If they are in pain, ask them to describe it and try to make them comfortable by supporting their head, neck, and back unless emergency services tell you otherwise.

Remember, the most important thing in an emergency is to stay calm, think clearly, and act quickly. By following these simple steps, you can provide basic first aid to someone in need and potentially save a life.

20. HOW TO DECIDE BETWEEN DOCTOR'S APPOINTMENT, URGENT CARE, AND EMERGENCY (ER) CARE

Navigating the world of healthcare can be confusing, but understanding the difference between medical facilities is vital to getting the right care at the right time, saving you time and money.

Doctor's Office:

Think of a regular doctor's appointment as your go-to for routine check-ups and minor health concerns. Whether combating a common cold, fighting the flu, or just needing a yearly physical, your doctor's office has got you covered.

Urgent Care:

Urgent care is your solution for health issues that can't wait but aren't necessarily life-threatening. Examples include a sprained ankle, a high fever, or severe abdominal pain. These types of issues need attention within 24 hours, making urgent care the perfect choice.

Emergency (ER) Care:

The emergency room should be your first stop when facing a serious or life-threatening condition. This includes things like chest pain, severe head injury, or severe bleeding. You don't want to waste any time when it comes to these types of situations.

How to Decide:

1. **Assess the severity**: If it's a matter of life and death, head straight to the ER. If it's not that serious but still requires prompt attention, an urgent care center is the way to go. And for routine check-ups or minor issues, make an appointment with your doctor.

2. **Consider wait time:** If time is of the essence, the ER is your fastest option. Urgent care may have a shorter wait time than a doctor's appointment, so keep that in mind as well.

3. **Cost**: A doctor's appointment is usually the most affordable option, while the ER is the priciest. Urgent care falls somewhere in the middle, so factor that into your decision-making. But you should always verify at the front desk based on your insurance.

Ultimately, it's always better to err on the side of caution regarding your health. Understanding the difference between these three types of medical facilities will help you get the proper care when you need it most.

PART FOUR
SMART SHOPPING FOR SMART EATING: MASTERING THE ART OF CHOOSING HEALTHY FOOD WHILE SAVING MONEY

21. HOW TO PICK PRODUCE FOR FRESHNESS

WITH THE EXORBITANT cost of groceries, no one wants to throw money down the drain by buying unripe or mushy fruit and vegetables that have to go into the trash. Despite the cost, it's essential to ensure you're eating colorful, fresh foods daily to get crucial micronutrients for strong health. Learning how to choose produce can seem overwhelming, but by following a few key tips, it's so simple you'll never select a bad piece of fruit again:

1. **Pay attention to color:** Choose produce with deep, rich colors, especially for fruits and vegetables with skin, such as cucumbers, squash, avocados, or eggplants. If there are bruises or discoloration, avoid it.

2. **Inspect the skin:** Check the skin of the produce for any bruises, soft spots, or discoloration. These are all signs that the produce may not be fresh.

3. **Know the right texture:** Fruits and vegetables should generally have a firm surface. If they're too soft, it's a sign that they may be overripe. If they're too hard, they'll likely have to sit for a few days before you can eat them. However, this varies by item, so be sure to know what you're looking for ahead of time.

4. **Be cautious of too beautiful:** Overly waxy, glossy, or 'perfect' looking fruits are also something to be cautious of – natural produce is often misshapen, and the colors aren't always the brightest. The opposite shows human additives, which could mean pesticides or chemicals.

5. **Seasonality:** Keep in mind that seasonal produce is often fresher and more flavorful than produce that's out of season. It's usually also cheaper. So if you're looking for the freshest produce, research online before heading to the store and opt for items in season.

6. **Trust your gut:** If it looks good, smells good, and feels good, chances are it is good. Trust your instincts when choosing produce.

7. **Don't be afraid to ask:** If you're unsure about the freshness of a particular item, feel free to ask the produce manager or a store employee for help.

22. HOW TO KNOW WHETHER TO BUY ORGANIC

Organic products can be expensive, but when it comes to your health, what price is too much? Even after washing non-organic produce before eating, 70% of fruits and vegetables still have residues of pesticides, chemicals used in farming to kill any organism that could damage the crop or land.[32]

Each year, a nonprofit organization called the Environmental Working Group (EWG) reviews laboratory tests on produce samples and releases lists to inform consumer health: the Dirty Dozen™ to summarize the 12 fruits and vegetables that have the highest levels of pesticide residues, and the Clean 15™ for those with the lowest.[33]

By prioritizing the purchase of organic products for the Dirty Dozen™ and choosing conventional produce for the Clean 15™, you can minimize your exposure to disease-causing pesticides while still keeping your grocery budget in check.

Here's how to use the Dirty Dozen™ and Clean 15™ to make informed decisions at the grocery store:

1. **Familiarize yourself with the lists:** The Dirty Dozen™ and Clean 15™ lists are updated annually, so make sure you have the most recent information. You can find the lists on the website of the EWG.[33]

2. **Prioritize buying organic for the Dirty Dozen**™: When shopping for produce on the Dirty Dozen™ list, choose organic products whenever possible to minimize pesticide exposure. It may be more expensive in the short term, but remember the potential long-term trade-offs to your health.

The Dirty Dozen™

The Clean Fifteen™

Terms trademarked by the Environmental Working Group, 2022 List.

3. **Decide what you want to prioritize for the Clean 15**™: For produce on the Clean 15™ list, it's okay to choose conventional or non-organic products, as they are less likely to contain high levels of pesticide residues. But if you want to buy organic, you know that what you're ingesting was grown in safe soil without synthetic pesticides or bioengineered genes (GMOs).[34]

4. **Consider other factors:** In addition to the Dirty Dozen™ and Clean 15™, other factors may influence your decision to buy

organic or conventional produce. You can also consider buying organic products if they are produced locally, if they are in season, or if they are grown using sustainable agriculture practices.

---

23. HOW TO READ EXPIRATION DATES

Imagine buying a brand new outfit for a big event, only to find out it's ripped or stained - that's how it feels when you buy expired food. All that excitement and anticipation for a delicious, home-cooked meal goes down the drain. Not to mention the money wasted! It's important to know how to read expiration dates to ensure the food you are consuming is safe and hasn't spoiled and to not flush your hard-earned cash down the toilet.

Here's how to read expiration dates in 4 simple steps:

1. **Know the different types of expiration dates**: There are three main types of expiration dates you should know:

- '**Sell by**' is the date the store must sell the product to ensure the consumer has time to use the product at home. You can still consume products 7-10 days after the listed 'sell by' date, but just be mindful of the limited consumption clock. If meat's sell-by date is fast approaching, it's best practice to freeze it as soon as you bring it home.
- '**Best by**' is the date that indicates when the food will have the best flavor and quality, its peak window of potency and freshness. It doesn't necessarily mean that the item is bad if past this date, although it may be. You'll have to use your senses to judge.
- '**Use by**' gives more information about quality than safety. These dates are chosen by the product's manufacturer, not safety regulators, and are particularly

common on beauty or skin products. Be aware of any product that has changed color or smell over time – if so, it's likely time to throw it out.

2. **Check the packaging:** Look for the expiration date. It should be easy to find and is often on the side or the back. All food products should have one, so do a brief check before putting items into your cart at the grocery store.

3. **Interpret the date**: Expiration dates are usually written in a month/day/year format. If the date has passed, it's best not to consume the food.

4. **Use your senses:** While the expiration date is a good guideline, it's also wise to trust your senses. Check the food's appearance, smell, and taste to ensure it's still safe to consume, particularly if getting close to the listed date.

24. HOW TO READ A NUTRITION LABEL

Think of a nutrition label as the blueprint for a food item - it shows you the ingredients and how much of each is included, just like a blueprint shows you what a building is made of and how it's constructed. By understanding a nutrition label, you can make informed decisions about what you're fueling your body with, just like a builder needs to understand a blueprint to construct a safe and strong building.

Learn the following to know with certainty what you put into your body with any given food item:

1. **Serving size:** Check the serving size first, as this information is used to calculate the rest of the values on the label. Make sure to compare the serving size to the amount you actually eat. For example, suppose the serving size says half. In that case, you'd need to double everything listed to understand what you would

actually consume in one serving. If the serving size is two, divide it by two.

2. **Calories:** This tells you the number of calories, or units of energy, in one serving of the food. Find your recommended daily calories based on age, gender, height, and activity level (you can look this up online). Then compare the number of calories listed to your total recommended intake. For example, if a snack package says 500 calories, and your recommended daily value is 2,000, you would have consumed 25% of your daily calories if you ate the entire bag.

3. **Macronutrients:** Look for the amounts of trans and saturated fats, cholesterol, sodium, and added sugars. Any items with large amounts of these should be avoided - they have far more health consequences than benefits. Look for total carbohydrates, fiber, and protein as necessary for your diet or specific dietary requirements.

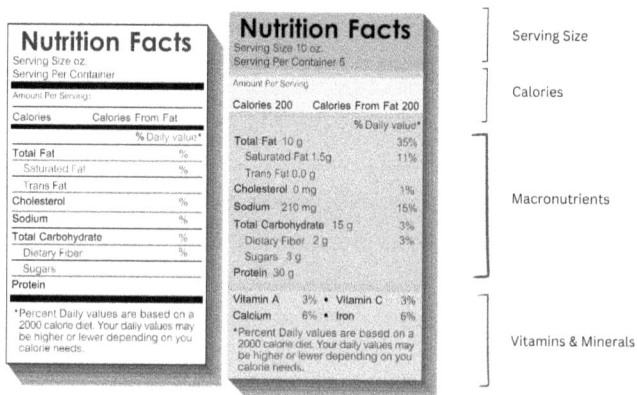

4. **Vitamins and minerals:** Check for the percentage of the daily value (DV) of vitamins and minerals such as vitamin A, vitamin C, calcium, and iron. You should consume 100% of the recommended values of all essential vitamins and minerals, so keep this in mind when you read a nutrition label.

5. **Ingredients:** The ingredients list is in descending order, so the first ingredient is the main one, and the last one is the least in amount. Look for whole, unprocessed ingredients, and avoid added sugars and saturated fats.

By taking the time to understand and interpret nutrition labels, you can make informed choices about the food you eat and support a healthy lifestyle.

25. HOW TO CALCULATE THE TRUE PRICE OF A PRODUCT: READING THE PRICE PER UNIT

When buying items in bulk, it can be difficult to tell if you're actually getting a good deal. Knowing the true cost of your purchases can help you stay within budget and make informed purchasing decisions. One of the best ways to determine the cost-effectiveness of a product is to look at its price per unit, also known as the price per ounce, price per pound, price per liter, etc. Let's say you're buying laundry detergent – how would you find out which one is the best value for the price?

1. **Find the total price and the unit of measurement:** Locate the total price of the product and the unit of measurement (such as ounces, pounds, liters, etc.) listed on the product label or shelf store. If referencing a shelf store price, read the price tag and ensure that the price listed references the product you're interested in and that the product wasn't in a misplaced location.

2. **Divide the total price by the unit of measurement:** To compare the price across different product offerings, you have to standardize what you're comparing to ensure that you compare the same unit. To do this, divide the product's total price by its units (ounces, pounds, etc.) The result will give you the price per unit of the product.

3. **Compare prices of similar products**: Compare the price per unit of similar products in the store to find the best value. This can be especially useful when comparing brands or generic items, as often times at first glance, it can seem like a particular product package is cheaper, but when you break it down, you may notice there's less volume actually included.

4. **Check for sales or discounts**: Don't forget to look for sales or discounts that might affect the unit price. Checking for special deals before making your final decision is always a good idea.

Whether you're shopping for a single item or making a weekly grocery list, understanding the price per unit is essential to help you save money and make the most of your budget.

26. HOW TO CUT ON COSTS AT THE GROCERY STORE

Going grocery shopping can be one of the largest weekly expenses. Being savvy with your expenses gives you more flexibility to save the extra or spend it on something fun. With a few simple steps, you can save money and still enjoy quality. Here are 6 easy ways to cut costs at the grocery store:

1. **Compare prices:** Before shopping, take a few minutes to compare prices at different stores. This can be as simple as a quick internet search to get a sense of what the average price is at different settings. You may find that one store consistently has lower prices for your needed items.

2. **Use coupons:** Coupons can be a great way to save money. Clip them from your local newspaper or search for them online.

3. **Sign up for a loyalty program:** Most stores also have loyalty programs that offer coupons and discounts. Some only offer their sale prices to loyalty members, so always be sure to sign up – 99% of the time, it's completely free.

4. **Buy non-perishables in bulk:** If you regularly use a certain item, particularly items that don't go bad (like deodorant or dishwashing soap), consider buying it in bulk. You'll save money in the long run and won't have to worry about running out as often. Just remember to calculate the unit price to get the best deal.

5. **Buy generic over brand name:** More often than not, the exact same item is more expensive when manufactured by a brand name. Go for the generic option if you look at the ingredient list and find no important differences.

6. **Stick to your grocery list:** Make a list of the items you need and stick to it. Impulse buys can add up; before you know it, you've spent much more than you intended.

PART FIVE
THE ART OF COOKING: USING KITCHEN APPLIANCES, UTENSILS, AND EXPERT TECHNIQUES TO CONCOCT DELICIOUS AND CREATIVE MEALS

27. HOW TO SAFELY USE KITCHEN KNIVES

WHETHER YOU'RE a seasoned cook or just starting out, knowing how to use kitchen knives safely is crucial. Losing your focus just once can spell disaster, and accidents are too prone to happen. The two keys to knife safety include properly holding a knife and proper use of a knife.

How to Properly Grip a Knife:

There are a few knife grips to learn, as they're best fit for different types of cutting and chopping.

1. **The Pinch Grip:** In this grip, you place your thumb and index finger on the blade, close to the handle, while the remaining fingers wrap around the handle. The pinch grip provides better control and precision for fine-slicing and dicing tasks.
2. **The Hammer Grip:** The name says it all – in this grip, you hold the knife handle with your whole hand, similar to a hammer. This grip is better suited for heavy chopping tasks.
3. **The Handle Grip:** The handle grip is when your whole hand is wrapped around the handle, with your index finger resting on top of the handle for added control. This grip is best for tasks that require more stability, such as cutting large vegetables or meat.

✗ Wrong   ✗ Wrong   ✓ Right

Practice with a dull knife, like a butter knife, until you feel comfortable with the grip. Even then, start slow, and err on the side of caution. Key motto: it's better to be safe and go slow than sorry and injure yourself, perhaps even permanently.

TIPS FOR SAFE KNIFE USAGE:

In addition to understanding how to hold a knife correctly, following these key safety tips whenever using knives in the kitchen is essential.

1. **Choose the right knife for the job:** Not all knives are created equal. Their shapes are designed with different functionality in mind. Choose the right knife for the task at hand to ensure safe and efficient cutting. For example, a chef's knife has a versatile blade that can handle various tasks. In contrast, a paring knife is designed for precision cutting with its small blade.

2. **Always use a cutting board:** A cutting board provides a surface to chop, dice, or mince food, which reduces the chance of the knife slipping. If using a board on a particular surface makes it unsteady, use a damp cloth underneath it to add stability. Never use a board that moves when you cut, and never cut without a board – not only will you damage the counter, but it's an accident waiting to happen.

3. **Cut away from your body:** When cutting, always move the knife in a direction away from your body, keeping your fingers curled and out of harm's way. Counterintuitively, not using dull knives can also help prevent many accidents from excessive force combined with slippage.

4. **Pay attention to what you're doing:** It's easy to get lost in thought while cooking, but focus must be maintained. Distracted cooking is one of the leading causes of knife accidents.

28. HOW TO USE THE OVEN

Nothing beats the convenience of cooking with an oven and having it do all the work for you. With the press of a button, you can leave your food alone and return to a deliciously cooked meal. But before using the appliance, it's essential to know the risks and how to stay safe.

Before Starting:

1. **Familiarize yourself with the controls:** The temperature dial or control pad will allow you to set the temperature, while the timer or clock will help you keep track of cooking time. You'll also see a button for broil, which uses direct heat from above, rather than all around, to cook your food. 'Clean' will heat up your oven to extreme temperatures that cause caked food to fall off the sides and reduce your need to manual scrub.
2. **Warm it up:** Preheating the oven before placing your food inside ensures it cooks evenly. Typically, recipe cook times refer to once the oven is fully preheated. You'll likely need to preheat the oven for at least 10-15 minutes before you start cooking. So, if you're hungry, remember to preheat before prepping your ingredients!
3. **Pick your rack:** Gas ovens usually have two or three racks. The lower rack is closer to the heat source and is best for dishes that need more heat from below, like casseroles or lasagnas. The upper one is farther from the heat source and is best for dishes that need more heat from above, like roasted vegetables. If you choose 'broil,' putting your dish on the top rack will put it directly under the blaring heat.

SAFETY TIPS:

1. **Be cautious of your dish material**: Use oven-safe dishes when cooking in the oven. Glass or ceramic dishes work best. Never put in plastic or synthetic materials, as these can melt and release toxic fumes.
2. **Set the timer:** Always use the timer so you don't accidentally forget about your food, which can lead to burning and fires.
3. **Check the food:** Keep an eye on the food as it cooks, and use a meat thermometer to check if it's thoroughly cooked. When monitoring the food while cooking, use the oven light instead of opening the door. This will keep the heat inside the oven, prevent the temperature from dropping, and reduce the unnecessary need to stick your hand in.
4. **Keep flammable items away:** Keep flammable items, like dish towels or oven mitts, away from the oven. You should always wear oven mitts for protection, but many are designed with flammable materials, so be sure that they never come into direct contact with a flame. Conversely, only buy entirely heat-resistant oven mitts.
5. **Steam alert:** Be careful of the release of hot steam when you open the oven door.

---

29. HOW TO USE THE STOVE TOP

You've probably already used the stove top to cook classics like mac'n'cheese, pasta, or soups and stews. Still, it never hurts to refresh on the basics, particularly when it comes to safety. Here are some things to be aware of when cooking on the stove:

1. **Know your stove top**: If you've ever used a gas stove, perhaps you've noticed one burner ignites sharply and

suddenly, while another always takes several tries. Familiarize yourself with the different burners and their respective heat outputs to prevent any risk of burning food or possible fires with open flames.

2. **Choose the right cookware:** Opt for pots and pans with flat bottoms the same size as the burner. Using cookware with warped or dented bottoms can cause uneven heating with food spillage from the sides.

3. **Adjust the heat:** Use the knobs to control the heat output, and start with low heat for delicate dishes and high heat for quick-cooking meals. Be careful about oil or liquids splattering at high heat that can cause burns.

4. **Keep it stable:** Place your cookware in the center of the burner and ensure it's stable to prevent spills from boiling.

5. **Don't leave anything near the stove while cooking:** Tea towels, clothes, and kitchen utensils can all be fire hazards if left near heat or open flame. Also, leaving a plastic utensil in your heated pot or pan can melt the plastic and release toxic chemicals into your food.

6. **Watch the handles:** As a best practice, always keep your pot and pan handles facing inwards, over the stove, so that they're more difficult to be accidentally pulled by a small child or to be hit and spilled.

7. **Keep a close eye:** Always stay near the stove while cooking to prevent fires and boilovers. Use a timer to keep track of cooking times and avoid leaving the kitchen while cooking.

8. **Turn it off:** When you're done cooking, turn off the burners and make sure all knobs are in the off position to prevent accidental fires. It's all too easy to take your food off the stove and forget to shut it off – don't waste your precious money on wasted electricity or gas or risk an accident!

9. **Keep it clean:** It can be tempting to leave it for another day, but clean up any spills or splatters immediately to prevent fires and to keep your stovetop looking its best.

---

30. HOW TO USE A GRILL

Whether you're a meat lover or vegetarian, there are all sorts of fun foods to make using a grill, and nothing quite beats that smokey taste! As with all cooking appliances, it's important to be knowledgeable in keeping yourself safe around heat and flames, so before tackling the grill on your own, be sure to do the following:

1. **Understand what type of grill you'll use**: Is it charcoal or gas? Charcoal is a bit more complicated as you'll have to light the coals and let them heat for about 20 minutes. Use a gas grill for a more convenient option. Gas grills use a propane tank and must be hooked up properly – reference the manufacturer's manual for specifics.

2. **Clean the grill:** Before each cook, clean the grates with a wire brush and oil them to prevent food from sticking. Never use soap, as this will affect the taste of your food! Water and a bristle brush will do just fine.

3. **Preheat:** As with the oven, you'll want to preheat the grill to ensure even cooking on all sides.

4. **Set the temperature:** Place the food on the grates and turn the heat on if you're using a gas stove. Depending on the type of food you're cooking, you may need to adjust the heat to medium or high settings. For example, a high heat is great for searing steaks, while a low heat is better for cooking chicken, vegetables, or ribs. If using a charcoal grill, you'll place the food directly over the heat for a stronger temperature.

5. **Monitor and flip when ready**: Flip only once or twice to keep maximum juices in the meat.

6. **Flavor:** Baste, or put your sauces or flavorings, on the meat just in the last few minutes of cooking – otherwise, it'll burn off.

And don't forget these key safety tips:

1. **Keep a safe distance:** Keep your grill at least 10 feet away from anything flammable, such as awnings, trees, or decks.
2. **Use long-handled utensils:** This will help keep you a safe distance from the heat and prevent accidental burns.
3. **Don't use utensils with uncooked juice on cooked foods:** This can cause cross-contamination and spread nasty germs that can get you sick.
4. **Keep a fire extinguisher nearby**: It's always a good idea to have a fire extinguisher nearby when grilling in case the unexpected happens.

31. HOW TO USE A SLOW COOKER

Once you live on your own or head off to university, you will likely have less time than expected to spend in the kitchen. Slow cookers may just become your new best friend. Slow cookers are different from pressure cookers as there's no pressure involved... a slow cooker uses insulated stoneware to heat enclosed food over a period of time. This handy appliance allows you to make hearty, home-cooked meals with little effort. You can simply add your ingredients, set the temperature and timer, and let the slow cooker do the work.

Whether making a savory pot roast, creamy mac'n'cheese, or a flavorful chili, a slow cooker is a versatile and easy-to-use tool that will make cooking a breeze. You can also use it for breaking down tender meats while keeping all the juices, and you can even use it to serve drinks like sangria or cider. Plus, with its safety features, such as the cool-to-the-touch exterior and automatic shut-off, you can use it with confidence, even if you're new to cooking.

1. **Choose the right recipe:** Pick a recipe designed for a slow cooker, as the cooking times, ingredients, and techniques are specially tailored for the appliance. You can find a variety of slow cooker recipes online or in cookbooks specifically for slow cookers.

2. **Prepare ingredients**: Cut vegetables, brown meats, and seasonings as instructed in the recipe, and then arrange them in the slow cooker in the order specified.

3. **Add liquids**: Pour in liquids such as broth or sauces as directed in the recipe.

4. **Cover and set:** Place the lid on the slow cooker and turn it on to the desired temperature and cooking time. Most slow cookers have low, medium, and high heat settings.

5. **Check and adjust**: Check the dish periodically and stir if required, or add more liquid if needed. Slow cookers tend to

cook evenly, so there's usually no need to do much adjusting. And one of its best features is that you can leave it on to cook while you do other things around the house.

6. **Serve and enjoy:** Once the dish is finished cooking, turn off the slow cooker and serve the food immediately or keep it warm on the "warm" setting until you're ready to eat.

Don't forget these key safety tips:

1. Always leave some clearance between the slower cooker and the wall it's plugged into – you don't want the hot surface directly touching another surface, or there's a risk of fire.

2. Keep it far from water sources: Electricity and water don't mix. So don't leave the cord hanging over the sink.

3. Always keep the slow cooker on a heat-proof surface, or else it could burn wood or melt the plastic.

Next time you crave a home-cooked meal but don't wait to put in the time, you now know about the understated joys of the slow cooker. Just remember to plan ahead since slow cooking takes time, but the result is well worth the wait!

---

32. HOW TO CHOOSE WHAT KITCHEN UTENSIL YOU NEED

As you start diving into cooking different foods for yourself, you may be overwhelmed by what seems like thousands of various tools and utensils to choose from. Kitchen utensils aren't cheap either, so here's how to decide which to spend your limited funds on and how to prioritize based on the ones you may use the most.

1. **Determine your cooking style:** Consider the dishes you like to prepare and what tasks you will perform in the kitchen. Will you

be sautéing vegetables or whisking sauces? Make sure to choose utensils that align with your cooking style.

2. **Consider the material:** Different materials have different properties and benefits. Stainless steel is durable and long-lasting, while silicone is non-stick and heat-resistant. Wooden utensils are great for gentle stirring and won't scratch delicate surfaces.

3. **Consider the size:** Consider the size of your pots, pans, and other cookware when choosing utensils. You want to make sure the utensil can reach all areas of the pan and won't get stuck or lead to you burning yourself.

4. **Think about storage:** Make sure to choose utensils that are easy to store. If you have limited cabinet space, consider utensils with holes or loops for hanging, or choose utensils that can be stacked.

5. **Always consider safety:** Never leave utensils in the pan or pot that still has the heat on – many plastics release cancer-causing chemicals, and wood utensils can catch fire. Remember to keep utensils used for raw meat separate from those used for non-meat to avoid cross-contamination.

---

33. HOW TO MAKE PASTA FANCY

Pasta is a staple food in many households and can often be considered bland or basic. But with a few simple tweaks, you can turn a boring plate of pasta into a gourmet meal. Here's how to make pasta fancy:

1. **Choose the right pasta:** Opt for unique shapes such as fusilli, rigatoni, or pappardelle. These shapes are perfect for holding sauces and spices, making your pasta dish more flavorful.

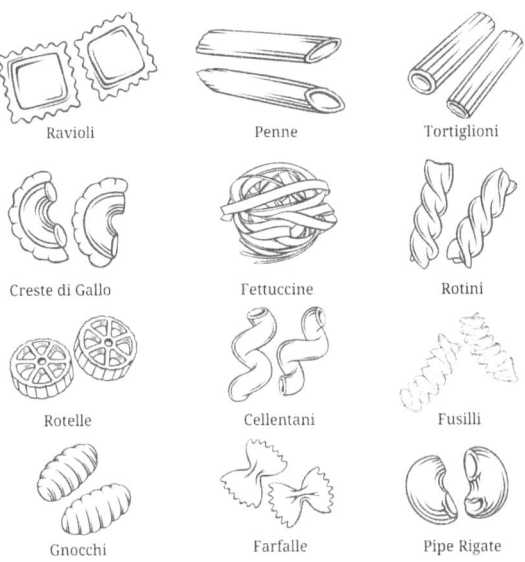

2. **Use fresh herbs:** Fresh basil, parsley, oregano, and thyme can instantly transform your pasta dish. Finely chop the herbs and sprinkle them over your pasta just before serving.

3. **Add some zing:** Lemon zest, chili flakes, or a splash of vinegar can add brightness and freshness to your pasta dish.

4. **Mix it up with veggies:** Adding fresh vegetables such as cherry tomatoes, mushrooms, or spinach can add texture, flavor, and nutrition to your pasta dish.

5. **Upgrade your sauce:** Make a fresh, homemade pesto or Alfredo sauce instead of store-bought tomato sauce. You can also add a touch of cream or cheese to your sauce to make it richer and more satisfying.

6. **Don't overcook your pasta:** Al dente pasta is key to any fancy dish. Overcooked pasta can become mushy and lose its shape, making it less appealing.

By following these tips, you can turn a simple plate of pasta into a gourmet meal that will impress your friends and family.

34. HOW TO MAKE SCRAMBLED EGGS LESS BORING

Eggs are a nutrient-dense food that provide a range of health benefits. They are high in protein, which helps with muscle growth and repair. They contain healthy fats that help with brain function and hormone regulation. And eggs are also a good source of vitamins and minerals such as vitamin D, choline, and selenium, which are important for overall health and well-being.[35]

Everyone loves scrambled eggs, but after having them for breakfast every day, it can get a little boring. Here's how to spice up this classic and make it more exciting:

1. **Experiment with spices:** Adding a pinch of salt and pepper to eggs is typical. Think outside the box with spices like cumin, paprika, and turmeric or herbs like basil or parsley. Add a dash to your eggs before beating them to find your perfect combination.

2. **Add cheese:** Grate some cheddar, mozzarella, or goat cheese into your eggs and beat them together. The cheese will melt, adding a creamy texture and extra flavor to your eggs.

3. **Add vegetables:** Chop up mushrooms, bell peppers, onions, or any of your favorite veggies and sauté them in a pan. Add your beaten eggs and cook them together until they are set. To

make it extra fancy, experiment with adding fried tomatoes and spinach to your eggs.

4. **Use cream or milk:** If you want your eggs to be extra rich and creamy, add a splash of heavy cream or milk to the beaten eggs before cooking. You can even use yogurt – just be careful not to add too much. And for a non-dairy option, instead of adding butter, try ghee – it tastes similar to butter, packed full of flavor but without the lactose that may upset your stomach!

5. **Top with toppings:** Serve your eggs with sauces like fresh salsa, hot sauce, chipotle sauce, or even pesto. Add in some avocado or smoked salmon for a protein-packed, satisfying breakfast.

35. HOW TO SUBSTITUTE WHITE RICE

White rice is quite common, but did you know it has the fewest health benefits compared to other rice grains? White rice is highly processed and has been stripped from its hull, the nutritious outer shell casing. For this reason, white reason contains many fewer vitamins and minerals than brown rice, for example. It also has a high glycemic index, which can cause blood sugar spikes and lead to a range of health problems, such as type 2 diabetes and obesity. Additionally, it's relatively low in fiber and lacks many nutrients found in whole grains. This can increase the risk of digestive issues and other health problems.[36]

So let's explore many other grains of nutrient-packed rice that are just as tasty, if not more so! Knowing the grains below is a great way to switch things up and add more flavor to your rice meals:

BROWN RICE:

- A healthy alternative to white rice, brown rice is rich in fiber and antioxidants, lowers the risk of heart disease, and manages blood sugar levels.[37]

- To cook on the stove, add 1 cup rice to 2 cups water; simmer for 45 minutes.
- Brown rice has a nutty flavor and chewy texture that pairs well with Asian-inspired dishes, grain bowls, hearty soups, and vegetable-based dishes.

JASMINE RICE:

- Known for its light buttery flavor, jasmine rice is often used as a base in curry dishes or sauteed with vegetables in stir-fry.

- To cook on the stove, add 1 cup rice to 1.5 cups water; simmer for 15 minutes.
- Jasmine rice's delicate, floral aroma and soft texture make it a perfect pairing for Asian dishes such as curries, stir-fries, and sushi, as well as tropical flavors like coconut, pineapple, and mango.

BASMATI RICE:

- Basmati rice has a bit longer grain than jasmine rice and is known for its aroma. It is commonly used in Indian and Pakistani dishes.

- To cook on the stove, add 1 cup rice to 1.75 cups water; simmer for 20 minutes.
- Basmati rice is perfect for Indian and Middle Eastern cuisine, particularly in dishes like biryani, pilaf, and curry, due to its long, slender grain and nutty flavor.

WILD RICE:

- Wild rice is known for its health benefits – it has three times the fiber of white rice and 30x more antioxidants than white rice.[37]

- To cook on the stove, add 1 cup rice to 4 cups water; simmer for 45 minutes.
- As a versatile grain with a nutty flavor and chewy texture, wild rice pairs well with dishes that incorporate earthy and savory ingredients such as mushrooms, herbs, and poultry.

36. HOW TO COOK MEAT LIKE A PRO

Cooking meat (if you eat it) is a valuable skill that opens up a world of culinary possibilities, allowing you to experiment with different cuts, techniques, and flavors. By understanding how to cook meat, you'll gain the confidence to prepare delicious meals for yourself and others while impressing your friends and family with your newfound expertise in the kitchen. Here's how to simplify the complexity that goes along with meat cooking:

1. **Choose the right cut**: Selecting the right cut of meat can make all the difference. Different cuts of meat have various textures, and therefore, a variety of cooking methods must be chosen from. For example, a steak should be grilled or pan-seared, while a roast is best roasted in the oven. As with all food, use your nose to approve for purchase or not.

2. **Allow meat to come to room temperature**: Take the meat out of the refrigerator at least 30 minutes to an hour before cooking. If frozen, it may need longer to dethaw. Not only does this

ensure that the cooking is even, but it also makes the meat juicier and tastier.

3. **Season well**: Season the meat with salt, pepper, or any other spices you prefer before cooking. A gentle seasoning helps to bring out the flavor of the meat, but don't feel like you need to go overboard – if it's good quality meat, you want the meat to speak for itself.

4. **Absorb extra moisture before cooking:** Direct contact between the meat and the hot pan allows for tastier caramelization (i.e. that brown-seared goodness) rather than steam from excess water, which inhibits the cooking.

5. **Don't overheat:** You want to ensure the meat is cooked thoroughly before eating, or else you can ingest bacteria that will make you sick. At the same time, you also don't want to overcook the meat, dry out all the juices, and leave yourself with chewy mouthfuls.

6. **Don't overcrowd the pan:** Don't overcrowd the pan when cooking meat. This causes the pan's temperature to drop and the meat to steam rather than sear.

7. **Let meat rest:** After cooking, allow the meat to rest for 5-10 minutes before cutting. This allows the juices to redistribute throughout the meat, rather than cutting it open too early and having the juices run down your plate.

PRO TIP - CLASSIC MARINADE PAIRINGS BY MEAT:

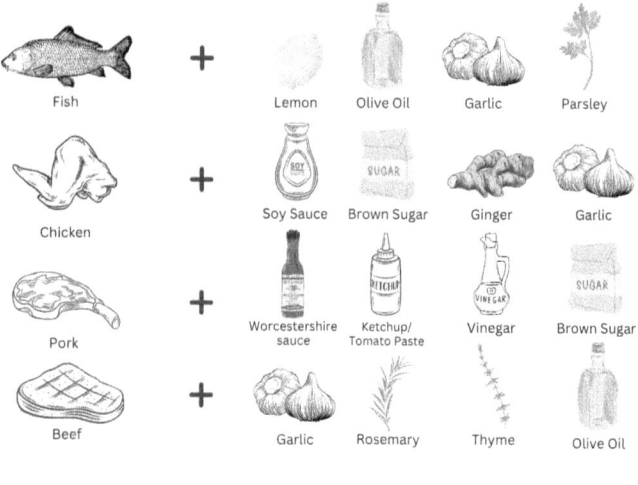

37. HOW TO MAKE SOUP FROM ANYTHING

Making soup is essential for getting started on your own – the ingredients are cheap, quick and easy to make in bulk and store for later, and convenient for carrying in a thermos on the go.

Follow these simple steps to make soup from anything you have on hand:

1. **Start with a base:** Begin with a basic broth or stock, such as chicken or vegetable. You can also use water if you don't have any broth on hand. Pro tip: look for low-sodium or organic for extra health benefits. Put in enough stock to cover the veggies.

2. **Add ingredients:** This can be anything from meat to pasta. Most soups are loaded with veggies, so add anything from broccoli to carrots to cauliflower or chickpeas and beans for something heartier. Your imagination is the limit! Cut everything into small pieces, trying a mix of big chunks and diced, and add it all to the pot.

3. **Get creative with spices:** Soup is an excellent opportunity to play with flavors. Use fresh or dried herbs, spices, and even

condiments to create a unique taste. Add olive oil, salt, pepper, and any spices you like (such as cayenne pepper, turmeric, or chili). Add tomato paste or canned tomatoes for a richer flavor.

4. **Experiment with textures**: Add some creaminess with coconut milk or cream, or create a chunky texture by adding diced potatoes or squash.

5. **Simmer it:** Let the soup cook on low heat for 20-30 minutes or until everything is cooked through and the veggies are soft.

6. **Blend it:** For a smoother texture, use an immersion blender to puree the soup or transfer it to a blender in batches.

7. **Garnish and serve:** Make your taste buds extra happy by garnishing some fresh cheese sprinkled on top or fresh herbs like basil or thyme. Ladle the soup into bowls and enjoy!

Making soup from anything is a great way to use leftovers, be creative with flavors, and enjoy a warm and comforting meal. Get creative and have fun!

38. HOW TO MAKE UNLIMITED INTERESTING SALADS WITH ONE BASIC FRAMEWORK

Whether you're looking to impress a date, whip up a quick and healthy meal, or simply expand your culinary repertoire, knowing how to make a salad is a valuable and versatile skill everyone should have in their back pocket.

Making a salad can be quite simple, yet constructing it using this painless framework provides infinite variability and allows you to build it to suit your tastebuds:

1. **Choose the base**: Pick a bed of greens such as lettuce, spinach, kale, arugula, or spring greens. Ensure to thoroughly wash

before eating, as greens can have insecticides, loose soil, and even insects on them – yuck!

2. **Add the body**: Assuming it's not a side salad, in which case you'd leave this part out. This is where the protein gets added, like egg, chicken, beans, or chickpeas. Aim to include at least 2 veggies (the most common are onion and tomato), and add a variety of colors and textures for aesthetics and flavor.

3. **Top with the head**: This is where you add your toppings, such as croutons, nuts, seeds, or dried fruits. Pro tip: these should complement the flavors of the body and add some crunch.

4. **Finish with the tip**: This is your dressing and the final touches that bring the salad together. Choose a dressing that complements your ingredients and drizzle it over the top. You can even add garnishes such as green onion or fresh herbs like parsley or cilantro for extra nuance in flavor.

5. **Toss and enjoy**: Mix everything together well before digging in!

---

39. HOW TO CREATE A SIGNATURE RECIPE

Cooking is an art form, and just like any artist, you can create your masterpiece by experimenting and adding your personal touch to the dish. A signature recipe is a great way to showcase your culinary skills and impress romantic interests, friends, and family. Here are some steps to help you get started:

1. **Choose your ingredients:** Start with ingredients you love and know work well together. Think about the flavors and textures you want to include in your dish. Perhaps they're unique and related to your heritage or a part of the world you have a connection to.

2. **Get inspired:** Look at recipes that are similar to what you have in mind and use them as a starting point. For inspiration, you can also look at cookbooks, food blogs, and cooking shows.

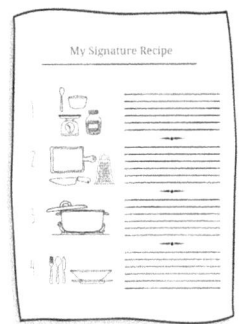

3. **Experiment:** Try different combinations of ingredients, cooking methods, and seasonings to find the perfect flavors. Focus on thinking outside the box of what's been done and what's to be expected with your ingredients and type of dish.

4. **Get creative:** Add your own unique twist to the recipe. You may want to incorporate a special ingredient, a favorite flavor, or an unexpected twist to the dish.

5. **Write it down:** Once you've found the perfect combination, write down the recipe, including the ingredients and their quantities, the cooking method, and any tips or tricks you used.

6. **Test and adjust:** Make your signature recipe several times to ensure the measurements and cooking method are just right. If needed, make any adjustments to the recipe until you're completely satisfied with the outcome. Consider not only the taste but the colors, textures, and aesthetics of presentation.

7. **Share and enjoy:** Share your recipe with your friends and family, and enjoy the compliments that come with it!

Creating a signature recipe takes time, patience, and a bit of creativity, but the end result is worth having a special piece of yourself to share with others!

40. HOW TO MEAL PREP

Meal prepping is an excellent way to make healthy and delicious meals for the week ahead. It's one less thing to do when you're hungry and tired in the heat of the moment. Plus, it saves you time and money.

1. **Plan your meals for the week:** Choose recipes for breakfast, lunch, dinner, and snacks for the week, and make a grocery list. Think about how you'll cook your meals in advance – do you batch cook all at once and then freeze, or will you put them into individual containers, ready to grab and go in the fridge?

2. **Shop for groceries:** Get all the ingredients you need for the week's meals. Aim to buy fresh produce, whole grains, lean protein, and healthy fats, and think particularly about ready-to-cook ingredients that will save you preparation time in the kitchen.

3. **Prepare ingredients:** If you need to prep any ingredients, it will save you time during the week to wash and chop vegetables, cook grains, and marinate meats in advance.

4. **Cook in bulk**: Cook meals in large batches, then divide them into individual portions. Store everything in airtight containers in the refrigerator or freezer, depending on when you plan to eat the food.

5. **Reheat:** When it's time to eat, simply reheat your prepped meals in the microwave or stove. You can also pack meals to go if you're on the move.

6. **Stay organized:** Label and date your prepped meals so you can track what you have on hand and when it needs to be eaten.

By meal prepping, you'll have healthy and delicious meals at your fingertips throughout the week, freeing up time and reducing the temptation to reach for junk food.

41. HOW TO PROPERLY STORE FOOD

Storing food properly is essential to keeping it fresh and preventing food-borne illnesses, which are more common than you may think. Here's how to keep your food and yourself healthy:

1. **Use airtight containers:** Transfer food from its original packaging to airtight containers or resealable bags to keep out air and moisture, which can cause bacteria to grow and, thus, food to spoil faster.

2. **Store food in the right place:** Different foods require different storage temperatures. Keep perishable items like meat, dairy, fruits, and vegetables in the refrigerator and pantry staples like

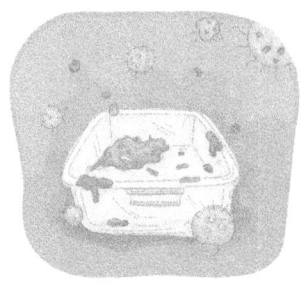
cereals, crackers, and spices in a cool, dry place.

3. **Keep raw and cooked foods separate:** Cross-contamination is a common cause of food poisoning. Store raw meats on the bottom shelf of the refrigerator so they don't touch or drip on other foods.

4. **Label and date food:** Label containers with the food item and the date it was opened or made to help you track how long it has been stored and prevent waste.

5. **Clean up spills in the refrigerator immediately:** Leaving open food spillage out is another place for bacteria to grow and spread.

6. **Keep all foods covered:** Leaving an unfinished, plated meal directly in the fridge can be tempting, but keeping it in the open tempts bacteria. The fridge's temperature can help slow growth but can't stop it completely; therefore, any covering automatically provides another barrier.

PART SIX
CLEAN LIKE A PRO: KEEPING YOUR HOME CLEAN, FRESH, AND INVITING WITH EASY CLEANING AND LAUNDRY HACKS

42. HOW TO AVOID DISASTERS IN LAUNDRY

DOING laundry is a tedious chore that most people would rather avoid dealing with. But learning to do laundry is an important life skill that can save time, money, and embarrassment. Imagine showing up to a date or an interview in a wrinkled, stained shirt or wearing socks that smell like the gym. Knowing how to do your own laundry can prevent these awkward moments and give you a sense of independence and self-sufficiency.

Here's how to keep your clothes looking new and smelling fresh:

1. **Read the labels:** Before throwing your clothes in the washing machine, read the labels. Different fabrics require different care, and the labels will specify what's needed. For example, some clothes can't be put in the dryer or else they'll shrink, and some need to be dry cleaned or they'll be ruined in the washer.

2. **Sort your clothes:** Sort your clothes into piles based on color – lights, darks, and mixed colors - and even by fabric type (e.g.,

denim). You don't want to mix your whites with your colored or dark clothes, as the colors may bleed in the washer.

3. **Pre-treat stains:** It's essential to put stain remover on a stain as soon as you see it, especially before putting it into the washer. This helps it soak deeper into the fabric to ensure all the grime comes out completely.

4. **Choose the right detergent:** Not all detergents are created equal, so choose depending on any skin sensitivities you may have. You also want to make sure the detergent is suitable for the fabric type – for example, with clothes that need to be washed on a 'delicate' setting, you will typically need to use 'delicate' detergent that is less abrasive and will cause less harm to the fibers.

5. **Use the right water temperature:** Different fabrics require different water temperatures, so be sure you're using the right one. Hot is typically best for extra-dirty clothing, but it's more prone to cause bleeding among clothes in the washer together. So for any clothes you have concerns about color bleeding, use a cool or cold setting.

6. **Choose the right setting:** You may also want to adjust your setting to a lower spin speed or a 'delicate' setting for more fragile fabric that you have concerns could rip or tear.

7. **Don't overload the machine:** Overloading the washing machine can cause your clothes to get tangled up and stretch. Washing your clothes in smaller loads is best, as it allows every item to be thoroughly cleaned.

8. **Dry clothes properly:** Once you've washed them, it's important to dry your clothes properly. When in doubt, use a setting with less heat, and go back to check the dampness frequently. Avoid over-drying, as this can cause shrinkage and damage to your clothes.

43. HOW TO IRON WITHOUT DESTROYING YOUR CLOTHES

Knowing how to iron your clothes is essential before an interview, a date, a big day at work, or anywhere you want to look your best! If done improperly, clothes can be burned and completely ruined, so follow these steps to be sure you are confident using the iron solo:

1. **Check the care label:** Before you start ironing, check the care label on your clothes. This will tell you the recommended ironing temperature and the type of iron to use.

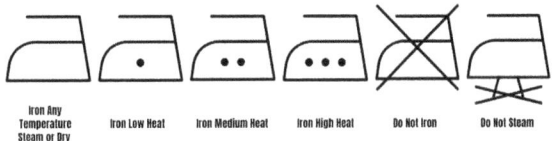

2. **Make sure the fabric is clean:** Wash and dry your clothes before ironing; otherwise, you risk deepening the stain and dirt into the fabric with heat. Ironing should be your very last step before wearing the clothing item.

3. **Use the right temperature:** Set your iron to the recommended temperature for the fabric type you're ironing. If unsure, start with a lower temperature and increase it if necessary. Otherwise, you risk burning the fabrics because the iron will be hotter than your selected setting.

4. **Use steam:** Steam helps remove wrinkles and freshen up clothes. Most newer irons have steam functionality and a place to insert a bit of water. Make sure you know the correct steam setting for your fabric type.

5. **Iron from the inside out:** Iron the inside of the garment first to avoid putting pressure on the outside and creating more wrin-

kles. Use the natural creases of the fabric for folding so that as you iron, you don't create new creases.

6. **Don't iron over buttons or zippers:** These parts can cause damage to your iron or your clothes. Iron around them instead.

7. **Use a press cloth:** If ironing delicate fabrics, use a press cloth to protect the material. You can use a clean, white cotton or a specially made press cloth.

44. HOW TO REMOVE TOUGH STAINS

Everyone wants their clothes and other items to look their best. Unfortunately, life is messy, and we'll inevitably get a tough stain somewhere along the way. But don't worry, there's hope, and you won't have to call your parents to figure it out! Here's how to remove tough stains:

1. **Identify the stain:** Before removing a tough stain, you need to identify what type of stain it is. Common tough stains include grease, oil, wine, blood, and ink.

2. **Act quickly:** The faster you act, the better your chances of removing the stain. The longer you wait, the more time the stain has to set in and become permanent.

3. **Gather your supplies:** You'll need a few things to remove tough stains - a clean cloth (white is better so there's no chance of color bleeding), a stain remover, and a basin of cool water.

4. **Apply the stain remover:** If you have a stain remover specifically designed for the type of stain you're dealing with, use it as directed. If you don't have a specific product, you can use white vinegar or a solution of equal parts water and dish soap.

5. **Blot the stain:** Gently dab the stain with your cloth, working from the outside in to prevent the stain from spreading.

6. **Rinse the fabric:** After you've removed as much of the stain as possible, rinse the fabric with cool water. Don't use hot water, as it can set the stain.

7. **Wash the fabric:** Wash the fabric as you normally would, either by hand or in the washing machine.

So what to actually use as a stain remover?

Beyond the typical products you can buy at the store, if you need a quick fix with something lying around the house, try these:

1. **Vinegar:** This wonder liquid is great for removing stains from clothes. Dilute it with water and apply it to the affected area before washing the garment as usual.

2. **Baking soda:** Baking soda is an excellent cleaner and deodorizer and can be used to remove stains from clothes. Mix it with water to form a paste, apply it to the stain, and let it sit for a few hours before washing.

3. **Lemon juice:** Lemon juice is a natural bleaching agent that can remove stains from white clothes. Apply it directly to the stain and leave it out in the sun to dry.

4. **Salt:** Salt can be used to remove stains from clothes, especially on fresh spills.

Simply sprinkle salt on the affected area, let it sit for a few minutes, and then rinse with cold water.

5. **Club soda:** Club soda is a great stain remover for clothes, especially red wine and coffee stains. Pour some club soda on the stain and blot it with a clean cloth.

45. HOW TO KEEP YOUR BEDSHEETS FRESH

Polls show that only about 20% of young people typically wash their sheets weekly, with most washing anywhere from every three to seven weeks![38] Weekly washing is recommended because there's all sorts of stuff that accumulates that we can't see – from dust to dust mites, to pet dander, to dead skin flakes, and dirt on your body from the day's happenings. While it's not necessarily something to be overly concerned about, nothing beats the feeling of lying down on clean, fresh sheets after a long day.

1. **Wash bedsheets regularly:** Commit to washing your bedsheets once a week, or every other week at most, to keep them fresh and free of any buildup of dirt, oils, or bacteria. This includes pillowcases. Make sure to use a gentle detergent on your skin and fabric.

2. **Choose the proper water temperature:** Choose the right water temperature for your bedsheet fabric type. Hot water is great for killing germs and removing tough stains but can also shrink or damage delicate fabrics. Cold water is gentler on fabric but may not be hot enough to kill germs or remove tough stains.

3. **Avoid fabric softeners:** Fabric softeners can build up on your bedsheets over time, making them feel stiff and reducing their ability to breathe. Opt for using natural fabric softeners like vinegar or baking soda instead.

4. **Store bedsheets properly:** Store your bedsheets in a dry place away from direct sunlight, fold them neatly, and place them in a drawer or on a shelf. You can also keep an extra set ready to go so that you always have sheets ready when washing.

5. **Invest in quality bedsheets:** Quality bedsheets will last longer, feel better against your skin, and keep you more comfortable at night. Look for sheets made of high-quality materials like Egyptian cotton, linen, or bamboo.

46. HOW TO UNCLOG A DRAIN

Picture this: you're taking a relaxing shower, enjoying the warm water washing away your stress. Suddenly, the water rises around your ankles, leaving you in a pool of soapy water. We've all been there, because clogged drains are quite common. Here's what to do to remove the drain on your own so it doesn't pile up:

1. **Boil Water:** Boiling a large pot of water can help to break down any grease or oils that may be clogging the drain. If that doesn't work, try it again but adding dish soap to the boiling water.

2. **Baking Soda & Vinegar:** Mix 1/3 cup baking soda with 1/3 cup vinegar and pour it down the drain. Let it sit for 15 minutes, then flush it with boiling water.

3. **Plunger:** Use a plunger to try to suction out any blockages. Fill the sink or bathtub with enough water to cover the plunger cup, then place the plunger over the drain and pump it vigorously up and down. Just ensure it's a clean plunger and not cross-contaminated from the toilet.

4. **Snake:** If the above methods do not work, you can use a drain snake to break up and remove the blockage. Insert the snake into the drain, turning the handle clockwise to feed the snake deeper into the pipe. When you feel resistance, keep turning the handle until the snake breaks through the clog.

If you're unable to unclog the drain, consider calling a professional plumber to help solve the issue.

47. HOW TO TURN OFF AN OVERFLOWING TOILET

One of the most terrifying experiences may be when the toilet is overflowing, you have guests over, and you don't know what to do. Don't panic! Do the following:

1. **Don't keep flushing:** This usually won't help and will only cause more water to be released and thus flood over and onto the floor.

2. **Locate the water shutoff valve:** This is typically found behind the toilet near the wall, and it's a small valve that controls the water supply to the toilet. If you can't find a shutoff valve, you may have an older toilet that uses a float. In that case, you'll pull off the tank to locate the float and ensure it's upright so it doesn't refill water into the tank.

3. **Turn off the water supply:** Turn the valve to the right (clockwise) to shut off the water supply to the toilet. Don't force it if it

won't turn; it's possible that the valve is rusty and that you'd need a tool.

4. **Flush the toilet:** Push down the handle to flush the toilet and let the remaining water drain out.

5. **Clean up the spill:** Use a mop or towels to clean up the water spilled from the toilet. This is important so that no water damage develops in the wet area.

By following these steps, you should have successfully turned off an overflowing toilet and prevented any further water damage. Remember to keep a plunger and a pair of gloves near the toilet so you're prepared in case of future overflow incidents.

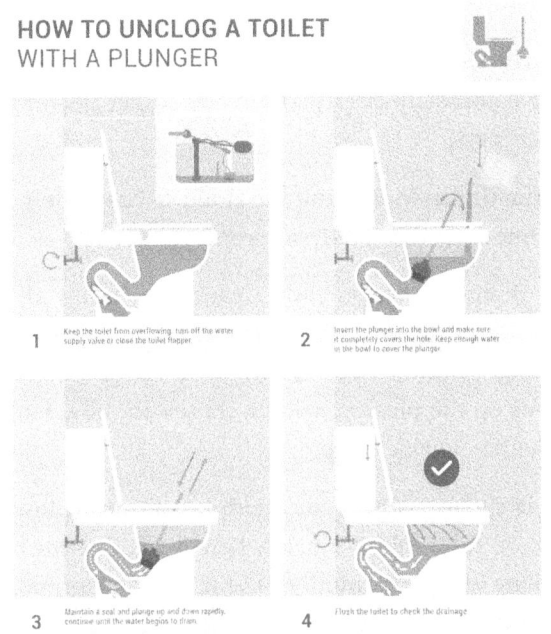

48. HOW TO DE-GRIME A SHOWER

Showers are the place where we start and end our day, but when grime and soap scum begin to build up, it can make us feel anything but refreshed. Cleaning a grubby shower is easier than it seems, especially if you stay on top of it by making it a regular part of your cleaning schedule:

1. **Gather supplies:** To get started, you'll need a cleaning spray, a scrub brush, and paper towels. If you have hard water buildup, you may also want to add a water spot remover to your list of supplies.

2. **Declutter:** Remove all shampoo bottles, soaps, wash clothes, and anything else from your shower. It should be completely empty and ready to get cleaning solution in all the corners.

3. **Clear the drain:** Make sure the drain is completely free from hair or grime so that it can drain properly.

4. **Spray it down:** Spray your cleaning solution all over the shower, paying extra attention to any especially dirty areas. Give the cleaning solution time to work its magic, following the instructions on the product you've chosen for how long it needs to be set before you clean up.

5. **Scrub it clean:** Using your scrub brush, go to town on any areas that are still grubby. The key here is to be gentle but persistent, working in circular motions to lift away the grime. You may have to apply another layer of cleaner to get it all out.

6. **Wipe the dirt away:** Use the squeegee if you have one or paper towels to wipe down the shower walls, removing any suds and streaks. Start at the top and work your way down, using gravity to your advantage, and soak up the grime with paper towels or cloth as you go.

49. HOW TO CLEAN A FLOOR THE RIGHT WAY

Even if there isn't dirt visible to the eye, our floors carry many more germs than we realize – pet fur, dust, dirt, and all sorts of disgusting stuff carried in from the bottom of our shoes and many other germ carriers, so it's absolutely essential to learn to clean floors properly.

Besides being hygienic, regular cleaning of floors is important for maintaining the integrity of the floors. Even if you're not yet a homeowner, you want to be sure to upkeep floors properly so that you're not charged a fee upon move-out by your landlord if repairs are needed.

Here are the steps to clean your floor the right way:

1. **Prepare**:

Understand your floor type: different surfaces need different cleaning materials. Remove any furniture or items that may be obstructing the floor. Vacuum or sweep the floor immediately before mopping to remove loose dirt and debris.

2. **Choose the right cleaning solution**:

Select a cleaning solution that is appropriate for your type of flooring. Avoid using solutions that contain harsh chemicals, as these can damage the surface of your floor. For general cleaning, a mixture of warm water and mild dish soap works well.

3. **Apply the cleaning solution**:

If using a traditional mop, fill your bucket with the cleaning solution and dip your mop into it. Wring out the mop so it's not too wet, or you may leave water spots on the floor. For steam mops, simply apply the disposable wet sweeping cloth.

Begin mopping the floor, starting from the farthest corner and working your way toward the door.

4. **Scrub tough stains**:

If there are any tough stains on your floor, you may need to use a handheld scrub brush to remove them.

Apply the cleaning solution directly to the stain and let it sit for a few minutes to release the hold of the stain before scrubbing it with the brush.

5. **Rinse the floor**:

After you've finished mopping, rinse the floor with clean water. Use a clean mop or cloth to remove any residual cleaning solution.

If using a steam mop like a Swiffer, you won't need to rinse the floor as a separate step, as the solution allows for cleaning and rinsing simultaneously.

6. **Dry the floor**:

Use a dry mop or cloth to soak up the excess water if very wet. Ensure the cloth is clean, or else you risk dirtying your newly cleaned floors!

You can also simply stay off the floor while it air dries. Avoid walking on the floor until it is completely dry, as this can leave footprints and streaks.

Allow the floor to air-dry completely before putting any furniture back in place.

Pro tip: Pick one or two days of the week that you'll commit to cleaning and making it a habit so that it gets done no matter what!

50. HOW TO KEEP THE REFRIGERATOR CLEAN

The refrigerator is the hub of the kitchen, where you store your food and drinks, and most of the time, it's easy to forget that it's a living, breathing machine that requires some upkeep. But keeping your fridge clean is essential not only for your health but also for preserving the life of your appliance. Here's how to keep your fridge squeaky clean and bacteria-free:

1. **Empty the refrigerator:** Remove all the food, condiments, and other items from the shelves and drawers. Check expiration dates and dispose of any spoiled or expired items.

2. **Clean the shelves and drawers:** Remove the shelves and drawers and wash them with warm, soapy water. For tough stains, try using baking soda and water or a plant-based cleaner. Make sure to dry them completely before putting them back in the refrigerator.

3. **Clean the interior:** Use a damp cloth or sponge to wipe down the interior walls, door, and gaskets. Don't forget to check the back of the refrigerator and the coils, which can accumulate dirt and dust.

4. **Organize the items:** After cleaning, you might as well add some organization - place the items back in the refrigerator while grouping similar items together and keeping frequently used items within easy reach.

5. **Set a cleaning schedule:** Designate a specific day each week or month to clean the refrigerator. This will help you stay on top of keeping it clean and catch any potential food safety issues before they become a problem.

PART SEVEN
HOME SWEET HOME: HOW TO FIND AND MAINTAIN YOUR PERFECT LIVING SPACE

51. HOW TO FIND THE RIGHT PLACE

MOVING into a new place can be an exciting and overwhelming experience, especially if you're on your own for the first time. You want to make sure you find a place that fits your lifestyle, budget, and needs. But where do you start? Here are some simple yet insightful steps to help you get started:

1. **Determine your budget:** Before you start your search, it's important to determine how much you can afford to spend on rent. Keep in mind that you'll also need to budget for utilities, internet, and other living expenses. You don't want to fall in love with a place only to realize later that you can't afford it.

2. **Know that price and location are intertwined:** Price reflects demand. So if you're looking in a higher-demand city or neighborhood of a city, you'll have to pay more. Typically living further out of a main hub will reduce housing prices.

3. **Make a list of must-haves:** What are the non-negotiable items you need in a living space? A parking space, close proximity to public transportation, in-unit laundry, or no pet fees? Make a list of these must-haves to guide your search.

4. **Start your search:** Use online resources such as apartment search engines, or ask your connections to keep their ears open for vacancies in their buildings. You can also express your interest at apartment complex leasing offices so that they reach out when openings become available.

5. **Visit properties in person:** Once you've found a few potential properties, make appointments to see them in person. This is a crucial step as it will allow you to see the place, meet the landlord, and get a sense of the neighborhood.

6. **Make a decision:** Trust your gut and choose the place that feels right for you and is within your budget. Don't be afraid to ask lots of questions and take your time to make a decision.

You'll be spending a lot of time in your new living space, and it will be your biggest expense, so it's important to make a decision you're comfortable with.

52. HOW TO APPLY FOR AN APARTMENT OR FLAT

So, now that you've found your ideal living space, you'll need to know how to start the rental application process. Don't worry; it's less daunting than it may seem:

1. **Ensure you meet the age requirements:** In most countries, individuals under the age of 18 cannot legally sign a lease or enter into a contract without the consent of a parent or guardian, be sure to check your county or local laws before moving forward.

2. **Gather necessary documents:** Before visiting potential apartments, ensure you have all the required documents to apply. This usually includes proof of employment and income, ID and address, previous addresses, previous rental history, and possibly even references. Check with the landlord or property management company to see what they require.

3. **Submit an application:** If you've found an apartment you like, it's time to submit an application, which you will often do in person at the leasing office. This will typically include a fee for a background check and a credit check.

4. **You may need a cosigner:** A credit check is run to assess your financial responsibility and how well you manage your money. It may also show that you haven't had much time to prove your financial responsibility. But if your credit score or income is too low, you may be required to find a cosigner, someone you know and trust who agrees to take responsibility for the rental agreement if you fail to make payments.

5. **Wait for a response:** Once you've submitted your application, you'll have to wait for a response. This can take anywhere from a few days to a few weeks. If your application is approved, the landlord or property management company will contact you with the details of your lease agreement.

6. **If approved, you'll be able to sign the lease:** Ask the landlord or property management company about the lease agreement and any additional fees. Ensure all your questions are answered and that the lease clearly documents all fees and agreements before signing.

53. HOW TO GET RENTER'S INSURANCE

Renter's insurance is a type of insurance policy designed specifically for renters that provides coverage for your personal belongings. It can help you protect your assets and keep you financially secure in case of theft, damage, or accidents. Some apartment complexes will even require you to show proof that you've obtained it, as their policies only cover damages to the buildings themselves. Here are some steps on how to get renter's insurance:

1. **Determine your coverage needs:** Assess what you need to protect, such as your furniture, clothing, electronics, kitchen items, and jewelry. The value of all of your belongings is probably much more than you think. This will help you determine the amount of coverage you need.

2. **Shop around:** Get quotes from different insurance providers and compare coverage and prices. Make sure to consider the reputation and customer service of the insurance provider as well.

3. **Read the policy details:** Once you have chosen a policy, thoroughly read and understand the policy details, including what is covered, what is not covered, and any limitations or exclusions.

4. **Choose a deductible:** A deductible is an amount you must pay first before insurance kicks in, while a premium is an insurance fee you regularly pay throughout the selected period. You will need to compare plans and decide on a deductible that works for you. A lower deductible typically means a higher monthly premium, while a higher deductible means a lower monthly premium.

5. **Get the policy:** Once you have chosen a policy, sign up for it and keep a copy in a safe place.

6. **Review your policy regularly:** Renter's insurance is a contract that you enter into, so review your policy regularly to ensure you have the coverage you need and that the policy is still up-to-date.

Ultimately, as the cost is relatively low to buy into a quality plan, renter's insurance may be just the move you never knew you needed to protect your personal belongings and give you peace of mind.

54. HOW TO GET ALONG WITH ROOMMATES

Moving in with roommates can be a fantastic opportunity to save money and make new friends, but it can also be a recipe for disaster if you're not careful. Consider who you'd like to live with carefully, and be sure to do the following no matter who you choose:

1. **Establish ground rules:** From the get-go, discuss and establish basic rules and expectations for cleanliness, quiet hours, visitors,

and whether you'll share food or any household items. This will help avoid any confusion or misunderstandings later on.

2. **Discuss bills and utilities:** As you'll have multiple utility bills, it's typically good practice for each person to put at least one bill in their name. This reduces the burden of one person being legally and financially responsible for everything if another refuses to pay. You can then discuss your processes for paying one another the difference and whether you'll pay rent together or separately.

3. **Split household duties fairly:** Assign household duties fairly, or take turns doing different tasks. This helps ensure that everyone contributes equally and no one person is overburdened.

4. **Respect each other's space and belongings:** Be mindful of your roommate's belongings and their personal space. Don't go into their room without asking, and keep common areas tidy.

5. **Communicate openly and regularly:** Good communication is key to a successful living arrangement. If you have an issue with something your roommate is doing, talk to them about it as soon as possible, and try to resolve it together.

6. **Be willing to compromise:** Living with others often requires some give and take. If your roommate wants to have friends over on a Friday night, try to be understanding and considerate, and ask for the same in return.

7. **Plan fun activities together:** Spending time together and doing things you all enjoy can help build a strong bond between roommates. Whether it's cooking dinner, playing video games, or watching a movie, find activities you all enjoy and do them together.

With these tips in mind, you should be able to build a positive and supportive living arrangement with your roommates. Living with others is about respect, compromise, and open communication.

55. HOW TO HANG A PICTURE

In the grand scheme of things, knowing how to hang a picture might not seem like a life-altering skill, but imagine the satisfaction of being able to display that epic concert poster or your own artwork without fear of it falling off the wall and hitting you in the head in the middle of the night.

And nothing quite makes a space feel like your own as when your decorations are hung on the walls.

Here's what to do to get it looking as if a professional did it:

1. **Gather your materials:** You will need your framed print, a hammer and nails, a measuring tape, painter's tape, a level, and a pencil. For heavier and larger items, you may need a picture hanger and a wall plug anchor. For lighter items, instead of nails, you may decide to use command strips.

2. **Measure the picture:** Measure the picture's length and width and note these measurements, so you know how to assess what section of wall space will work.

3. **Choose the location:** Decide where you want to hang the picture and measure the height at which you want to hang it. Usually, slightly above eye height while standing is the height to go for. Keep in mind the height of the furniture and any other items in the room that might obstruct the view of the picture.

Think also about keeping it in line, or intentionally out of sync, with other wall hangings or decorations.

4. **Install the hardware:** Use the measuring tape and pencil to mark the spot where you want to place the nail or hardware. If you need hardware, install it according to the instructions provided and ensure it is level using the level.

5. **Hang the picture:** Attach the wire to the hooks or nails, and then attach the picture to the wire. Ensure the picture is straight and level, and adjust the wire if necessary.

And that's it! You now have a beautifully hung picture that will bring some life to your living space.

---

56. HOW TO FIX A HOLE IN THE WALL

Accidents happen, and sometimes, a hole ends up in the wall. No need to worry; fixing a hole in the wall is a simple and straightforward process, especially when using caulk. With a few tools and materials, you'll have that hole fixed in no time:

1. **Clean the area:** Use a dry cloth to remove any loose debris, dust, or dirt from the area surrounding the hole. This will ensure the caulk adheres properly.

2. **Apply the caulk:** Squeeze a small amount of caulk into the hole, being careful not to overfill it. Use a putty knife or your finger to smooth the caulk and align it with the wall surface.

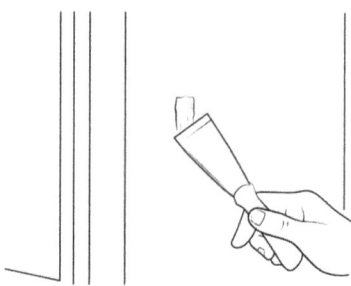

3. **Allow the caulk to dry:** Let the caulk dry according to the manufacturer's instructions. This usually takes a few hours.

4. **Sand the surface:** Once the caulk is dry, use sandpaper to smooth the wall's surface around the hole. Remove any excess caulk and create a smooth, even surface.

5. **Paint over the caulk:** Finally, paint over the caulk to match the color of the surrounding wall. Use a small brush or roller and apply a thin, even coat of paint. Let the paint dry completely.

Remember, it may take a bit of time and patience to get the repair looking perfect, but with a little bit of effort, you'll be able to fix that hole, and your landlord will never know!

---

57. HOW TO CHANGE THE BATTERIES IN A SMOKE ALARM

Imagine waking up in the middle of the night to the sound of a piercing alarm. The room is filled with smoke, and you can't see anything. It's every tenant's nightmare, but it's a scenario that you can prevent by learning how to change the batteries in your smoke alarm, one of the most important safety devices in your home:

1. **Locate the smoke alarm:** Start by finding all smoke alarms in your home. They are usually located on the ceiling or near the ceiling and in each bedroom, kitchen, and living room area.

2. **How to know if the batteries need changing:** Batteries should be changed immediately if they're chirping or have blinking lights. You should also consistently check the batteries every month so that you're well aware in advance of any low or dying batteries.

3. **Remove the smoke alarm cover:** To access the batteries, you'll need to remove the cover from the smoke alarm. Simply press the tab or unlock the mechanism and gently pull the cover down.

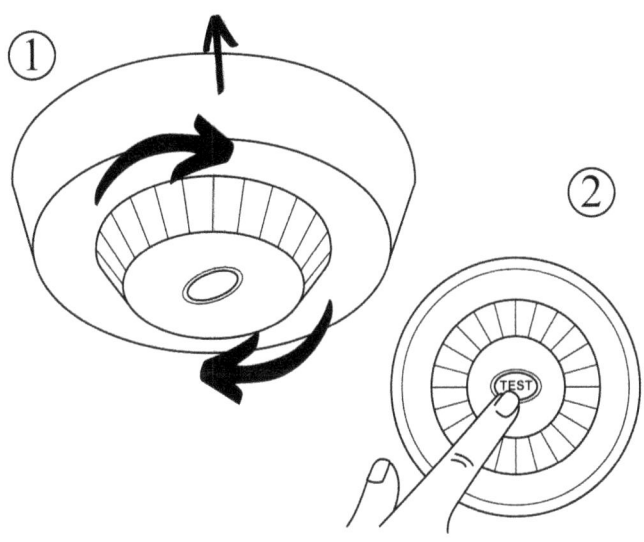

4. **Replace the batteries:** Once you can access the batteries, simply replace the old ones with new ones. Ensure the batteries are the correct size and type for your smoke alarm.

5. **Reattach the cover:** Once the batteries are in place, reattach the cover to the smoke alarm by pressing it back into place.

6. **Test the smoke alarm:** Finally, turn the power back on and test the smoke alarm to ensure it works properly, which you can do simply and safely be pressing the test button to trigger the alarm.

PRO TIPS:

1. It's a good idea to discuss fire safety plans and who's responsible for changing the batteries with your landlord or property manager before signing the lease.

2. There should be a minimum of one smoke alarm in an apartment, but ideally one per bedroom, on every level of the home, and in main living areas. Be sure to ask or check before signing a lease.

58. HOW TO USE A FIRE EXTINGUISHER

Fire extinguishers can be intimidating, but they can also be the difference between a small fire and a life-threatening disaster. Knowing how to use a fire extinguisher properly could save your life or the lives of others, so it's important to be prepared.

In the case of a fire, you should always evacuate and call your emergency services. It's still important to know how to use a fire extinguisher in the case of very small fires where you have an extinguisher readily available, but only if you feel confident in using one and have a clear escape route. If any of these criteria aren't met, never stay where a fire is breaking out to fight it. If you ever feel uncomfortable in any way, always evacuate immediately, no matter how small the fire is.

Here are the simple steps to use a fire extinguisher if the fire is still small and controllable. You can remember the acronym PASS, which is often taught in fire safety: [39]

Step 1:
Pull the pin

1. Pull the pin: The pin locking mechanism prevents the handle from being accidentally pressed. To use the fire extinguisher, simply pull the pin out.

2. Aim the nozzle: Point the nozzle of the fire extinguisher at the base of the fire.

3. Squeeze the handle: Squeeze the handle to release the fire-extinguishing agent. The handle is usually located near the bottom of the extinguisher.

4. Sweep from side to side: Move the fire extinguisher from side to side in a sweeping motion, making sure to cover the entire area of the fire.

5. Keep a safe distance from the fire and avoid inhaling the fire-extinguishing agent. Put your safety first and call emergency services when in doubt.

PART EIGHT
ON THE MOVE: MASTERING SKILLS FOR SAFE AND CONFIDENT TRAVEL

59. HOW TO GET AN OIL CHANGE

CHANGING the oil in your car may not sound exciting, but it's one of the most important things you can do to keep your vehicle running smoothly and prevent costly repairs down the road.

If you want to change your own oil, you can, but if you don't mind paying, it'll save you time and grime to get it done by a professional. Here's what to do to get your car's oil changed:

1. **Determine when you need an oil change:** Check your vehicle's owner manual to determine the recommended oil change interval or look for the 'change engine oil' message or light that may appear on your vehicle's information display.

2. **Choose a reputable service center:** Look for a service center that specializes in oil changes, or choose a dealership that sells your make and model of vehicle. Pro tip: Many service centers have oil change coupons available online – scope it out before paying full price!

3. **Schedule an appointment:** Call the service center to schedule an appointment for an oil change or use their online booking system. You can also drive up, but you may need to wait a bit for cars that arrived first.

4. **Prepare for the appointment:** Gather your vehicle's registration and insurance information, and ensure you have a way to get home if the appointment will take a long time.

5. **Arrive at the appointment:** If you made an appointment, get there on time and let the service advisor know you are there for an oil change.

6. **Choose your oil:** You'll be asked whether you want to use conventional or synthetic oil. Synthetic oil is a man-made, high-performance lubricant that can provide better engine protection and last longer than conventional oil, but it typically comes at a higher cost. Conventional oil is simply made from crude oil. If you don't know what type you need, you can simply ask the mechanic for their recommendation and ask why they suggest that specific oil type.

7. **Wait or leave:** Choose to either wait at the service center or leave and return later to pick up your vehicle. It typically doesn't take more than 10-20 minutes, so usually, it's worth waiting.

Stay on top of your oil changes, and never keep extensively driving your car when the oil change light comes on to keep your car engine happy and running smoothly!

60. HOW TO FOLLOW AN AUTO MAINTENANCE SCHEDULE

Learning to follow an auto maintenance schedule is essential because it helps keep your car running smoothly and safely and can also help prevent more costly repairs down the road. A well-maintained car will have a longer lifespan, perform better on the road, and have a better resale value. Regularly following the recommended maintenance schedule can also help to identify and address potential issues before they become bigger problems.

1. **Preparatory information:** Identify the make and model of your car, as well as the year it was manufactured. This information will help you determine the specific maintenance schedule for your vehicle.

2. **Find the maintenance schedule**: Check your car's manual or manufacturer's website for the recommended maintenance

schedule. This schedule will detail the services and inspections recommended for your car at specific mileage intervals.

3. **Track the upcoming service date:** Keep track of your car's mileage and note the next service due based on the schedule.

4. **Keep up with oil changes**: Take your car in for regular oil changes and other routine services, as the schedule recommends.

5. **Maintain records:** Keep a record of all maintenance and repair work performed on your car, including dates, services performed, and costs.

6. **Keep an eye and ear out for deviations from the norm:** Don't ignore warning signs or sounds from your car, such as a warning light or unusual noise. Get it checked out promptly, as it may indicate a more serious issue.

7. **Keep up with routine maintenance:** Schedule regular inspections, such as tire rotations and brake checks, to ensure your car remains in good condition and performs at its best.

By staying on top of your car's maintenance, you can get the most out of your investment and avoid unexpected and costly repairs.

61. HOW TO GET CAR INSURANCE

Getting car insurance for the first time can seem overwhelming, but it's an important step in protecting yourself, your vehicle, and others on the road – and it's required by law!

1. **Determine your coverage needs**: Consider factors such as your state or locality's minimum insurance requirements, the value of your car, and your budget to determine how much coverage you need.

2. **Shop around:** Get quotes from multiple insurance companies to compare coverage options, prices, and discounts.

3. **Review your policy:** Make sure you understand what's covered under your policy and any exclusions or limitations.

4. **Provide required information:** You will likely need to provide your driver's license number, vehicle information, and personal information to obtain car insurance.

5. **Pay and complete the process:** Once you've chosen a policy, you'll need to pay your first premium and complete the process. You will then receive an insurance card to keep in your car for proof of coverage.

6. **Review your policy regularly:** It's a good idea to review your policy regularly to ensure you have the coverage you need and to take advantage of any discounts or savings opportunities.

By following these steps, you can make getting car insurance for the first time less daunting and ensure you have the protection you need to feel safe and protected every time you hop in your car. It's one of those things that you want to be absolutely sure that you have before any chance of actually needing to use it.

62. HOW TO PUMP GAS

Pumping gas for the first time is a rite of passage for all new drivers. It can seem confusing before you've done it, but in reality, it's a simple and straightforward process. Follow these steps:

1. **Determine the type of gas you need:**

Before pulling up to the gas station, check your owner's manual to determine the type of gas your car requires. You'll typically find this information in the "Fuel" section. Most cars use regular unleaded gas, but some require premium or mid-grade fuel. Using the wrong type of gas can damage your engine and decrease your car's fuel efficiency.

2. **Pull up to the gas pump:**

Once you've determined the type of gas you need, it's time to pull up to the pump. Choose a pump that's easily accessible and not already in use. The standard etiquette is that, if there are two open pumps in the same row available, to pull forward towards the furthest one. This allows a car that arrives after you to easily get gas behind you, rather than having to pull forward and back up.

3. **Turn off your engine:**

It's absolutely critical to turn off your engine before pumping gas to prevent any accidents. Sparks from the engine could potentially ignite the gasoline from the pump if not, so always make sure your car is all the way off before pumping.

4. **Pay for your gas:**

In most cases, you will have to pay before you're able to pump any gas. You can either use a card with the set up at the pump, or with cash, you can go into the gas station to pay with the clerk, just make a note of which pump number your car is it (there will be a big, numbered sign above each pump).

5. **Open your gas tank:**

Locate your gas tank door, which is usually on the side of the car where the gas cap is located. There is typicall a button or lever inside of your car that you have to press first, before you can then twist off the cap to the gas tank.

6. **Select the gas grade and pump:**

Select the gas grade that matches your car's fuel requirement. You'll find the different grades of gas listed on the pump's dispenser. Place the nozzle inside the gas tank opening and press the handle. Most gas pumps have a lever that allows you to lock the handle in place for hands-free pumping. Don't overfill the tank, as this can cause gas to spill out.

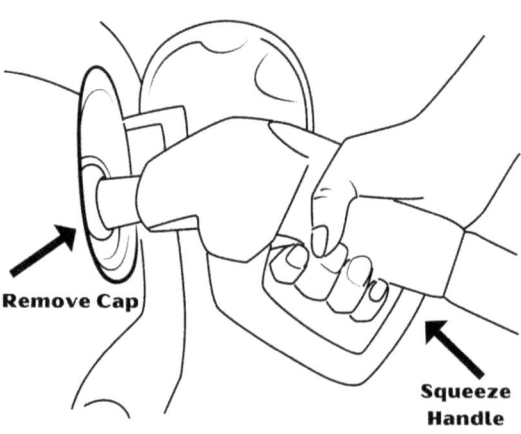

7. **Be sure to close your gas tank properly:**

Make sure you don't drive off with your gas tank open! It's not the end of the world if so, it happens. But be sure when you take the pump out of you tank that you remember to twist the cap back tightly on your tank.

SAFETY NOTES:

1. Always make sure to turn off your car's engine while pumping gas, and never smoke or use your cell phone near the pump. This is essential to reduce any risk of fire. Gasoline is highly flammable and can ignite if exposed to a spark or an open flame.

2. Turning off the engine eliminates the possibility of sparks from the starter or alternator, and not smoking or using a cell phone eliminates the risk of fire from a lit cigarette or electrical spark from your phone. Keeping a safe distance from potential sources of ignition protects you, your vehicle, and the gas station and its customers.

---

63. HOW TO USE JUMPER CABLES

Knowing how to use jumper cables can be a lifesaver, both figuratively and literally. Imagine being stranded on the side of the road with a dead battery and having the ability to jumpstart your car and get back on the road. Not only is it convenient, but it can also save you the hassle and cost of calling for a tow truck. Plus, helping someone else in need with a jump is a great way to be a Good Samaritan. So, learning this simple yet valuable skill is important for every driver, especially those just starting to drive.

1. **Locate the batteries**: Find the batteries of both the dead car and the car that will jumpstart it. Make sure both batteries are easily accessible and in close proximity.

2. **Check battery compatibility:** Make sure the batteries are compatible. Some batteries require special cables that may not be included in a standard set of jumper cables.

3. **Connect the cables:** Connect one red cable to the positive terminal of the dead car battery and the other red cable to the positive terminal of the working battery. Connect one black cable to the working battery's negative terminal and the other black cable to an unpainted metal surface in the engine compartment of the dead car.

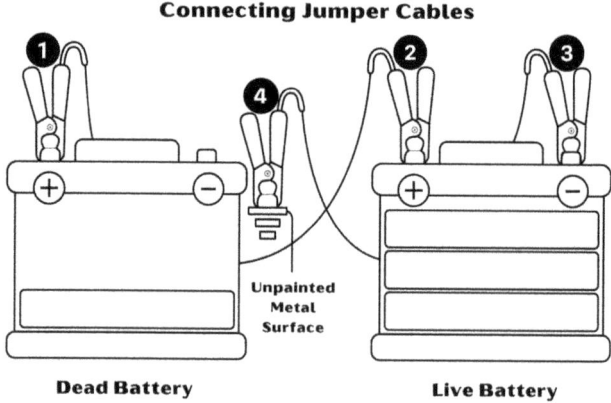

4. **Start the working car:** Start the car with the working battery and let it run for a few minutes. This will allow the alternator to charge the dead battery.

5. **Start the dead car:** Try starting the dead car. If it starts, remove the cables in the reverse order of how you connected them. If it doesn't start, wait a few more minutes and try starting it again.

6. **Disconnect the cables:** Once the dead car has started, it's important to remove the cables in the reverse order of how you

connected them. This helps prevent any sparking or damage to the engine.

It is important to note that using jumper cables correctly is crucial to avoiding damage to your car's electrical system and ensuring safety for yourself and others. If unsure, it's better to call a professional or a trusted, knowledgeable source.

64. HOW TO DEAL WITH A CAR ACCIDENT

Road traffic accidents are the 8th leading cause of death for people around the world. In the United States, road traffic injuries are the number one cause of death for young infants through people in their mid-50s.[40][41] Therefore, you must take all the safety precautions you can, such as wearing a seatbelt, following the speed limit, not getting in a car with someone inebriated, and not driving at night or on poorly light roads when it can be avoided.

Although you are the type of person who will be as safe as possible while in a vehicle, it is still important to know what to do in a car accident to stay safe and protect your rights.

1. **Stop your vehicle:** As soon as you're involved in a car accident, stop your vehicle as soon as it is safe. Failure to stop after an accident is a crime in most states.

2. **Check for injuries:** Check yourself and any passengers for injuries, and call 911 immediately if anyone is injured. If the accident is minor and everyone is safe, you can skip this step.

3. **Move your vehicle:** If your car is still functional, and it's in the middle of the road or a hazard to other drivers, move it to a safe location, pulled over to the side, but still in the location in which the accident happened (i.e., you don't want to drive miles down the road, unless it's important for your and others' safety).

4. **Exchange information:** Gather information from the other driver, including their name, address, phone number, insurance company, and policy number. Also, write down the make and model of the other vehicle and its license plate number, and make a note of the intersections or roads in which the accident happened.

5. **Document the scene:** Take photos of the damage to your vehicle and the surrounding area, and note the conditions at the time of the accident. All of this will be asked of both you and the other driver by the insurance companies.

6. **Report the accident:** Call your insurance company to report the accident. Be sure to give them all the information you have gathered, including the other driver's information and any photos or notes you took at the scene.

7. **If you don't have insurance, you must pay out of pocket**: Remember that if you don't have car insurance, you will have to pay for damages to your car and the other out of pocket, and you may even be heavily fined. Always insure your car, because you just never know what may happen.

Knowing what to do in a car accident can help you stay safe and protect your rights. By following these steps, you can ensure that you handle the situation in the best way possible. Just remember to stay calm and take the necessary steps to ensure everyone is safe.

65. HOW TO KEEP YOUR COOL WHEN BEING PULLED OVER BY POLICE

Have you ever seen flashing lights behind you while driving and felt a sense of unease? Being pulled over can be an intimidating experience, but it's important to know what to do to stay safe and protect your rights. Here's a simple guide on what to do when you get pulled over.

1. **Pull over safely:** As soon as you see the lights, turn on your hazard lights to indicate that you are pulling over, then find a safe and legal spot to stop, out of the way of other driving cars.

2. **Stay calm:** Take a deep breath and stay calm. Turn off the ignition and keep your hands on the steering wheel where the officer can see them. Don't reach for any ID until the officer tells you to do so.

3. **Provide license and registration:** The officer will ask for your license and registration. It's best to keep them in an easily accessible spot, such as in your glove box, so you can quickly hand them over. Out of an abundance of caution, inform the officer what you're doing whenever you move your hands off the steering wheel.

4. **Answer questions:** The officer may ask you questions about why you were pulled over and what you've been doing. Answer truthfully in a polite and respectful tone, but don't volunteer any unnecessary information. Let the officer do the talking, and keep your answers simple.

5. **Never consent to a search:** If the officer has legal grounds to search the car, they will search it whether you give your permission or not. So never give consent willingly, but inform them politely and respectfully that you do not consent to a search.

6. **Keep composure:** If you disagree with the reason for the stop, don't argue with the officer. Wait until you can speak to a lawyer or attend a court hearing to dispute the citation.

7. **Follow instructions:** Finally, follow the officer's instructions and sign any citations they issue. Remember that you have the right to remain silent and can choose to exercise that right at any time.

Being pulled over by the police can be a nerve-wracking experience, but by staying calm and following these steps, you can ensure a safe and smooth encounter. By knowing your rights and responsibilities, you can help protect yourself and handle any potential legal issues that may arise.

66. HOW TO BUY A TICKET FOR PUBLIC TRANSIT

Public transit is a great way to save money and help the environment, and it may just be your only option in a big city if you don't yet have a car. However, if you're new to public transit, buying a ticket can seem like a daunting task. But don't worry, it's actually pretty simple:

1. **Determine the type of ticket you need:** Before buying a ticket, you need to determine what kind of ticket you need. Different public transit systems may offer different types of tickets, such as single-ride, daily, round-trip, weekly, or monthly. Choose the one that best fits your needs. Weekly and monthly passes are generally cheaper per unit ride, but only buy it if you'll use it frequently enough to be worth it.

2. **Find the ticket vending machine:** Once you know what type of ticket you need, it's time to find a ticket vending machine. These machines are typically located at transit stations or on buses and are easy to spot. Look for a machine with a sign that says 'tickets' or 'fare.' Some public transit systems also let you buy online or through an app, so do some research to see if that's an option.

3. **Choose your ticket type:** When you reach the ticket vending machine, select the type of ticket you need. The machine should have clear instructions and buttons to help you choose the right ticket.

4. **Insert payment:** Once you've selected the ticket type, insert your payment into the machine. You can usually pay with cash, debit card, or credit card.

5. **Retrieve your ticket:** Once you've paid, the machine will dispense your ticket. Take it, and you're good to go!

6. **Use your ticket:** Show your ticket to the transit operator when you board the bus or enter the train station. Or you may have to swipe the barcode or tap it as you pass through a subway or metro gate. Keep your ticket with you in case you need to show it again.

---

67. HOW TO READ A MAP OF PUBLIC TRANSIT

Getting around a new city or even your own city can be tricky, especially if you are trying to navigate using public transit. But reading a map for public transit is not as complicated as you think, and with the right tools and techniques, you'll be a pro in no time:

1. **Identify your starting point:** Take note of your current location on the maps around the transit station or inside the bus or subway. This will help you know where you are in relation to your destination.

2. **Locate your destination:** Identify your end destination on the map to see the best route to take.

3. **Find transit lines:** Look for the lines on the map that represent the area's different modes of public transit. These lines will be color-coded and labeled with the mode of transit they represent, such as a subway line, bus line, or train line.

4. **Plan your route:** Decide which transit line you need to take to get from your starting point to your destination, making a note of the stations you'll need to transfer at, if necessary. In general,

particular routes of transit lines are labeled with their final point running in that direction. Once you understand this naming method, you'll easily know which direction of the line is right for your route.

**BOSTON
RAPID TRANSIT**

5. **Check schedules and stops:** Make sure to double-check the schedules of the transit lines you'll be using and the stops along the way. This way, you'll know when to expect your ride and where to catch it.

6. **Take note of transfer points:** If you need to transfer from one line to another, take note of the transfer points and give yourself enough time to get from one line to the other.

So many smartphones these days make it super simple for you: you can simply use your GPS to plug in your start and end location; when you choose the public transit option, it'll then show you exactly what stop to get on at, what stop to get off at, and all the stops in between!

68. HOW TO USE RIDE SHARES SAFELY

Ride shares, like Uber and Lyft, are a convenient way to get from place to place without having to drive yourself. However, it's important to know how to use these services safely. Here are some key safety tips:

1. **Order your ride from indoors:** Avoid waiting outside and looking down at your phone, particularly at night, for tens of minutes while you order and wait on your ride. You only need to go outside as your track the driver and see that they are pulling up or just a minute away.

2. **Verify the driver and the vehicle:** Before getting into a rideshare, check the driver's name, photo, and license plate to ensure it matches the information provided by the ride-share app. You should also check reviews and ratings when a driver is assigned, and feel free to drop the ride and request a new one if they don't seem legit.

3. **Always sit in the back seat opposite the driver:** You want to take the furthest spot from the driver to ensure there's the most space between you both as possible.

4. **Keep your information confidential:** There's never a need to share any personal details.

5. **Let someone know your plans**: Let a trusted friend or family member know your plans, including the driver's name, vehicle make and model, and your intended destination. This can help ensure your safety in case of an emergency.

6. **Use the in-app safety features:** Most ride-share apps have safety features, like sharing your trip details with a trusted contact or an emergency button to contact local authorities. Be sure you know how to use these features in case you need to.

7. **Trust your instincts:** If you feel uncomfortable or unsafe for any reason, don't hesitate to decide not to get into the car, or if already inside, to ask the driver to pull over or to end the ride. Trusting your instincts can be one of the most important steps in staying safe while using a ride-share.

8. **Always wear a seatbelt:** Always wear your seatbelt while in a ride share, no matter how short the trip may be.

PART NINE
MONEY MATTERS MADE EASY: LEARNING THE WEALTH-BUILDING BLUEPRINT FOR LIFELONG FINANCIAL FITNESS

69. HOW TO SAVE YOUR HARD-EARNED CASH

SAVING money is a critical life skill that will serve you well throughout your life. It can be challenging, especially when there are so many things you'd like to buy. So why is saving money even important? Becoming someone who saves money regularly will give you more independence, teach you the value of your work compared to the cost of items, and provide you a cushion for unexpected expenses.

With a bit of discipline, patience, and the right strategy, you can learn how to save your hard-earned cash and make your money work for you.

1. **Set a goal:** Start by setting clear and specific financial goals. This could be saving up for an emergency fund to afford your first apartment, your first car, to buy a pet, or to go to university. Having a clear target that feels exciting and rewarding will help you stay motivated and focused on your saving efforts.

2. **Avoid impulse purchases:** Avoid impulse purchases like the plague – this is the number one drain of money for young people! Wait at least 24-48 hours before making any big purchases. Reflect over the next few days whether you truly want and need to purchase that thing by asking questions like, "Do I already have something similar?" or "Will this purchase bring me long-term joy?" Consider the trade-offs for your longer-term savings goals.

3. **Use a savings mobile app:** There are many tools readily available to help you track your progress. Make a note of your goals and how much you save in reality per paycheck, per week, or per another time period. Assess how you're doing and be honest with yourself.

4. **Automatically save any monetary gifts:** For example, birthday or graduation money should be saved, not spent. Put

that money aside towards your long-term goals like college or a new place. Instead spend a small percentage of your job earnings towards things you want but don't necessarily need (key word 'small').

Learning to save money is one of the most important skills you can develop as a teen. It not only helps you take control of your finances, but it also prepares you for the future. By saving your hard-earned cash, you can build a strong financial foundation to give you the peace of mind and stability you need to pursue your dreams and goals.

BEFORE MAKING ANY PURCHASE, ASK YOURSELF:

 1 "Do I need this?"

 2 "What am I giving up if I buy this?"

 3 "Why do I feel like I need this item?"

 4 "Have I waited 24 hours?"

70. HOW TO BUILD LONG-TERM WEALTH WITH COMPOUND INTEREST

Starting to build wealth at an early age can be a great way to secure your financial future. One of the best ways to do this is by taking advantage of the magic of compound interest. It may sound dry and boring, but its power to make you wealthy without much effort on your part at all cannot be overstated.

Compound interest is when you earn interest not only on your original savings but also on the interest you have already earned. This can lead to a significant increase in your savings over time.

Take the following two examples: [42, 1]

1. **Someone who is 15 years old:** They start investing in the S&P 500 at $100 a month and continue until age 65. Their total returns are $793,172, while their direct contributions were only $60,000. That's a *$733,000 gain* just from compound interest alone!
2. **Someone who is 25 years old:** They start investing $100 a month and continue until age 65. Their total returns are $349,100, while their direct contributions are $48,000. That's a *$301,000 gain* from compound interest – less than half of the first scenario!

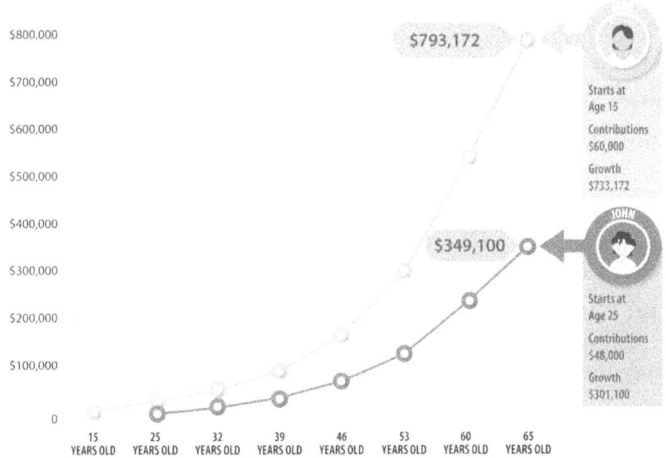

Here's how to build wealth with compound interest:

1. **Start early:** The earlier you start saving, the more time your money has to grow. Even small amounts of money can add up to

a substantial sum over time with the help of compound interest. As the proverb goes, "The best time to plant a tree was 20 years ago; the second best time is now."

2. **Invest in a high-yield savings account:** Look for a savings account that offers a high-interest rate. This will allow your money to grow faster as you earn interest on both your original savings and the interest you have already earned. Most interest rates at common banks are only around 0.01%, which means you only get $1 of interest for every $10,000 you save! Compare that to an interest rate of 4%, in which you'd get $4 for every $100 saved – that's a massive difference!

3. **Be consistent:** The key to building wealth through compound interest is to consistently save and invest over a long period of time. Set up automatic monthly contributions to your savings account so you don't have to think about it. Remember, it's paying your future self first!

4. **Take advantage of compounding frequency:** The more often interest is compounded, the faster your money will grow. Choose a savings account that compounds interest daily or monthly rather than annually.

---

71. HOW TO BUDGET FOR BEGINNERS

Saying goodbye to living paycheck to paycheck and hello to financial stability starts with budgeting. Budgeting allows you to take control of your finances and make the most of your income. It also ensures that you don't spend more as you earn more and throw all that valuable extra income down the drain. It's never too early (or late) to start, and the good news is, it's a lot easier than it sounds:

1. **Know your income:** The first step in budgeting is understanding how much money you bring in each month. Make a list

of all sources of income, including your job, side hustles, and any other sources of cash flow.

2. **List your expenses:** Make a list of all your monthly expenses, including rent, utilities, food, transportation, entertainment, and any other regular bills. Don't forget to include occasional expenses such as birthdays, holidays, and car maintenance.

3. **Categorize expenses:** Group similar expenses together, such as housing, food, and transportation. Make note of the essential expenses, those that are necessary for survival, and those that aren't, meaning 'wants' rather than 'needs.' This will help you get a clearer picture of where your money is going. The 'wants' bucket should be as low as possible.

4. **Allocate your money:** Now that you have a list of your income and expenses, it's time to allocate your money and decide where it needs to go every month (or another time period you specify). Subtract your expenses from your income and determine how much you have left over each month. If you don't have any remaining, this means you may be short on bills, or at a minimum, that you have no money to take care of your future self through saving and investing.

THE 50-30-20 BUDGETING RULE

50% Essentials (Bills)

30% Non-essentials ('Wants')

20% Saving & Investing

of Your Total Income

5. **Make adjustments:** If you find that your expenses are greater than your income, it's time to make adjustments. Look at areas where you can cut back, such as entertainment, clothing, or eating out, and prioritize necessities like groceries, school supplies, and affordable housing and transportation.

6. **Track your spending:** Finally, it's important to track your spending to ensure you're sticking to your budget. You can use a simple spreadsheet, budgeting app, or even just a piece of paper to keep track of your spending.

Remember, budgeting is a process and takes time to perfect. Be patient, stay committed, and make adjustments as needed. With a budget in place, you'll be on your way to financial stability and a brighter financial future!

72. HOW TO HAVE YOUR CREDIT SCORE HELP NOT HARM YOU

Understanding how to use credit effectively is crucial for financial success, especially as you begin building your life and making important decisions. With a 'good' or 'excellent' credit score, you get:

- **Better loan options:** A good credit score can help you qualify for better loan terms and lower interest rates, which can save you a lot of money in the long run.
- **Improved financial flexibility:** With a good credit score, you have more options to finance large purchases, like a car or a home, and can do so on favorable terms.
- **Peace of mind:** Knowing how to use credit wisely can help you feel more confident and in control of your finances, giving you peace of mind in the present and future.

- **Future opportunities:** Good credit is often necessary for things like starting a business or buying a home and could even impact getting a job (although this is not the norm).

To keep your credit score on your side so that it helps rather than harms you, here's what to do:

1. **Check your credit report:** It may vary by country or locality, but you can generally check your credit for free once per year. It's important to obtain a copy of your credit report at this interval and check it for any errors or possible identity theft, meaning a stranger is using your credit as their own. Dispute any errors you find with the credit reporting agency.

2. **Always pay bills on time:** Late payments harm your credit score, so it's important to make payments on time. Set up automatic payments or reminders to ensure you never miss a payment. This shows banks you're trustworthy to lend money to, reflected in a higher score.

3. **Limit credit card usage:** Using too much credit can hurt your credit score, so limit your credit card usage to 30% or less of your available credit limit.

4. **Avoid applying for too many loans or credit cards:** Each time you apply for credit, it can result in a hard inquiry, which can negatively impact your credit score. Try to limit the number of loan and credit card applications you make.

5. **Keep old credit accounts open:** This helps to increase your average account age, which is a positive factor in your credit score. So instead of closing accounts you don't use, keeping the account open actually works to your advantage.

By following these tips, you can help ensure that your credit score works in your favor and not against you. Your credit score is an important factor in your financial future, so it's important to learn how to maintain and use it to your advantage.

73. HOW TO UNDERSTAND THE PROS AND CONS OF CREDIT CARDS

Credit cards can be a convenient way to make purchases and build credit, but they also come with massive risks that can impact your life trajectory if not used responsibly. Understanding the pros and cons of credit cards is crucial for making informed financial decisions.

1. PROS:

- **Convenience**: Credit cards allow for easy and convenient purchases without having to carry cash.
- **Rewards**: Many credit cards offer rewards such as cashback, points, or miles for purchases made on the card.
- **Builds credit**: Using a credit card responsibly can help build and maintain a good credit score, which comes into play when you need to borrow money for a home, car, or business.

2. CONS:

- **High-interest rates**: If not paid in full, credit card purchases can accrue high-interest rates, leading to debt. Interest rates for credit cards typically fall in the 20% range, meaning the amount you owe stacks up

dramatically and can increase much more quickly than your ability to pay it off. This traps many people in a cycle of debt that is extremely difficult to break free of.
- **Fees**: Late payment fees, annual fees, and over-the-limit fees can add up quickly.
- **Temptation to spend**: It can be easy to overspend with a credit card and end up in debt.

3. KEY TAKEAWAYS:

- Always pay your credit card balance in full each month to avoid interest charges.
- Read the terms and conditions of a credit card before applying to understand any fees or restrictions. There are many details about fees, penalties, and high-interest rates in fine print that are purposefully not clearly communicated to consumers.
- Limit the number of credit cards you have and only use credit when necessary. Only sign up for a credit card with parental permission and oversight to slowly build credit and get the hang of paying off your card fully and on time. But if you ever doubt your ability to pay off a card, it's better to use cash or a debit card, which directly reflects the amount of money you have in your bank account.

Using credit wisely can lead to financial stability and success, but misusing it can lead to debt and harm your credit score.

74. HOW TO OPEN A BANK ACCOUNT

Beginning to manage your finances as a teen is a crucial step toward financial stability and independence. Having a bank account is an excellent place to start. It helps you keep track of your money and make transactions safely and securely. Here are the steps to follow when opening a bank account:

1. **Determine your needs:** Ask yourself what kind of account you need, a savings account or a checking account, and what type of features you want, such as online banking, mobile banking, and overdraft protection. A checking account is typically used when you need access to your funds more frequently, as unlimited deposits and withdrawals are usually allowed, while savings accounts are for holding money more in the medium to long term. Some banks only offer a certain number of monthly withdrawals from a savings account before you have to pay a fee.

2. **Research banks and compare options:** Research different banks in your area and compare their fees, interest rates, and services to determine the best fit for your needs. Be sure to understand how many deposits and withdrawals are allowed, what the fees are for withdrawing from an ATM that is not theirs, and if there are any monthly maintenance fees or if you have to keep a minimum amount in the account without being charged.

3. **Gather required documentation:** To open a bank account, you'll need a government-issued ID, proof of current address, and a social security number or equivalent. If you're under 18, you may also need a parent or guardian to co-sign the account.

4. **Schedule an appointment or visit a branch:** You can visit a bank branch or schedule an appointment to open your account. During the appointment, you'll need to provide the required documentation and complete the necessary paperwork. Typically you'll have to make an initial deposit as well.

5. **Set up online banking:** Once you have your account set up, you can then set up online banking and mobile banking services to access your account from anywhere, at any time.

---

75. HOW TO DEPOSIT AND WITHDRAW FUNDS IN A BANK ACCOUNT

Once you have a bank account, you'll want to be sure you understand how to access your money. There are now multiple ways to deposit and withdraw funds based on what works best for you:

In-person at the bank:

1. Find a nearby bank branch or ATM to make a deposit.
2. Fill out a deposit slip with your account information and the amount you want to deposit. Note that some banks no longer require this step as long as you have your bank card and ID with you.
3. Insert your cash or checks into the designated slots in the drive-thru, or simply hand them over to the teller if you went inside.
4. Confirm the details from the teller and retrieve your receipt – it's as simple as that!

Through the mobile application:

1. Download and log into your bank's mobile app, ensuring you always keep your username and password safe (safety tip: don't automatically save your details, but memorize them so only you can access them).
2. Tap the 'deposit' feature and select the account you want to deposit to.
3. Input the amount of cash you want to deposit.

4. Take a picture of the front and back of the check, and be sure to sign on the line.
5. Confirm the details and submit the deposit.
6. Keep the check or cash in a secure location until it clears.

76. HOW TO MONITOR A BANK ACCOUNT BALANCE

Monitoring your bank account balance helps you keep track of your spending and understand where your money is going. It also helps you avoid overspending, prevent overdraft fees, spot fraud or transaction errors, and plan for your future.

1. **Familiarize yourself with online banking:** Get to know the ins and outs of your bank's online platform so you can check your account balance anytime, anywhere.

2. **Set up balance alerts:** Many banks allow you to set up balance alerts to notify you via text, email, or push notification when your balance reaches a certain amount. This way, you can catch overspending early on. You can also set up alerts that let you know if you have reached the maximum transfer or withdrawal limit (usually applies to savings accounts only).

3. **Keep track of transactions:** Regularly check your transaction history to see where your money is going. This will help you make informed decisions about your spending and keep your balance in check.

4. **Schedule regular balance checks:** Make it a habit to log into your account regularly to stay on top of your finances. This can be daily, weekly, or monthly, depending on your preference and spending habits. Consistently open and read your monthly bank statements to keep an eye out for any erroneous charges or double transactions and maintain a solid understanding of your

financial situation. Having this knowledge will allow you to make more informed decisions about your spending, avoid overspending, stay within your budget, and build financial stability.

77. HOW TO WRITE A CHECK

Checks may seem outdated, but they're actually still used in many scenarios, such as in paying rent to a landlord or mailing in your payment on a bill. Being able to write a check is a valuable life skill that you'll use for years to come:

1. **Gather the necessary materials:** Before you begin, you'll need a checkbook, a pen, and the information of the person or business you're paying.

2. **Fill in the date:** Write the current date in the top right corner of the check.

3. **Write the recipient's name:** Write the name of the person or business you're paying in the 'Pay to the Order of' line. This information must be correct, or they may not be able to receive your payment.

ANATOMY OF A CHECK

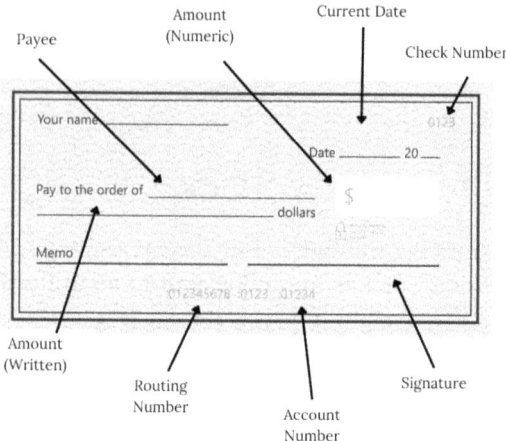

4. **Write the dollar amount:** Write the amount of the check in numbers in the small box and in words on the second line under the name. With any leftover space after you've written the amount, write a line through it so no one could theoretically write something else in. Make sure the two amounts match.

5. **Fill in the memo line:** This line is optional, but you can use it to write a reminder of what the check is for. Often, you'll need to write your apartment number here if you're paying rent or your account number if paying a bill.

6. **Sign the check:** Finally, sign the check in the bottom right corner. Make sure you sign the check the same way you did when you opened your account.

78. HOW TO PAY BILLS ON TIME WITH AUTOMATIC PAYMENT

Automatic payments can ensure bills are paid on time, reducing the risk of late fees and improving credit scores. It's one less to-do task out of your brain, but it's important to be sure that you always keep enough in your account, or else you risk an overdraft fee.

To pay bills on time with automatic payments set up online, follow these steps:

1. **Identify which bills you want to pay automatically:** This may include utility bills, rent/mortgage payments, credit card bills, etc.

SET UP AUTO PAYMENTS

2. **Find the company you want to pay and navigate to their online payment portal**: You will need to set up an online account if you don't already have one.

3. **Enter your account information and payment details**: Enter in your identification and payment details, such as the amount you wish to pay and the payment method (usually a debit or credit card). Only use a card you are sure you will have enough money in or can pay off, or you risk racking up fees and incurring debt.

4. **Set up automatic payments:** Select the option to set up automatic payments and specify the frequency and amount of payments.

5. **Review and adjust:** Review the details of your automatic payment setup and make any necessary adjustments.

6. **Submit:** Confirm the automatic payment setup and make sure you receive a confirmation email. The last thing you want is to

think you're making automatic payments, but they never actually go through.

7. **Regularly check the automation:** Monitor your bank account to ensure the automatic payments are made as scheduled.

PART TEN
YOUR CAREER LAUNCHPAD: A COMPREHENSIVE GUIDE TO DEVELOPING PROFESSIONALISM IN THE WORKPLACE

79. HOW TO APPLY FOR A JOB

LANDING your first job can be a big step towards independence, self-discovery, and financial stability. Still, it can also be intimidating, especially if you don't know where to start. That's why it's important to approach job applications with confidence, organization, and a bit of research, just like a detective gathers evidence to solve a case. With the right skills and approach, you'll be able to impress potential employers and find the job that's the perfect fit for you:

1. **Understand age requirements:** You'll need to be familiar with the laws of your locality to be sure you meet the legal age for work. For example, in some areas, no employment is allowed for 15 year old's or younger, but some allow it with a restricted number of weekly hours.

2. **Get a work permit if needed:** You should also check your locality, but in most cases, if you are under 18, you will need a work permit to be allowed to work. This is meant to protect minors from exploitation.

3. **Find your references:** Reach out to trusted contacts you've interacted with in some professional capacity in the past, whether a volunteer supervisor, coach, teacher, or mentor, and ask for their approval to speak on your behalf if requested as you search for employment.

4. **Research online or scope out in person:** Before you apply, research the company or organization you are interested in working for. This will help you tailor your resume and in-person expressions of interest to their needs and show the interviewer you are serious about the job. You want to also be sure that the location is accessible to you and that they'll be flexible around your school schedule.

5. **Prepare your resume:** Update your resume to include your skills, experience, and education relevant to the job you're applying for. Make sure it's well-structured and easy to read. Not all entry-level jobs will require a formal resume outside of their standard application, but it doesn't hurt to have one – in fact, it will make you stand out from the crowd and look very professional!

6. **Apply online or in-person:** Most companies now allow you to apply online through their career websites or job boards such as LinkedIn. If the company prefers in-person applications, dress appropriately and bring a copy of your resume and cover letter.

7. **Follow up:** After submitting your application, follow up with the company to show your continued interest in the position. A polite email or phone call makes all the difference in securing an interview!

---

80. HOW TO BE SUCCESSFUL IN AN INTERVIEW

So, you've landed an interview for your dream job and want to make a great impression? Follow these tips, and you're nearly guaranteed success:

1. **Research the job:** You want to not only have a strong understanding of the duties laid out in the job description, but you also want to research the company and learn as much as you can about its products, services, values, and culture. Pro tip: when you reflect on how your values align with the organization's values during an interview, you become a top-tier candidate.

2. **Prepare answers:** Spend some doing some deep reflection on your strengths, areas for improvement, your greatest accomplishments, career goals, and skills that you have to bring to the table. Your thoughtfulness in responses beyond the basic

responses many people give will shine through in the interview and set you apart.

3. **Practice:** This is different from preparation. Beyond planning what you would highlight as your strengths, achievements, goals, and so forth, you should practice communicating them - speaking it aloud clearly, concisely, and confidently is a separate skill.

Interview Prep Checklist

- ☑ Why do you want this job?
- ☑ What is your greatest strength?
- ☐ What is your greatest weakness?
- ☐ Tell me about your last job.
- ☐ How would previous supervisors describe you?
- ☐ Tell me about a conflict in your last job and how you handled it.
- ☐ Where do you see yourself in 5 years?
- ☐ Why should we hire you?

Pro Tip: Focus on clarity, concision, & confidence!

4. **Dress appropriately:** The standard rule is to always dress one level more formally or professionally than your interviewer will be dressed. You want to portray your professionalism as if you were already working for the company. This shows that you respect the company and the interviewer.

5. **Be on time:** Arrive 10-15 minutes early for the interview to allow for unexpected events, such as traffic. This also shows that you respect the interviewer's time. Even being one minute late

will dock against you in the typical interviewer's eyes. Early is on time.

6. **Show enthusiasm:** During the interview, be enthusiastic about the company and the job opportunity. Smile, make eye contact, and listen actively. Focus on making a human connection with your interviewer.

7. **Ask questions:** Prepare a few questions to ask the interviewer about the company and the role. This shows that you're interested, engaged, and thoughtfully reflecting on your fit in the role. You don't just have to save your questions for the end, although that's typical. If it makes sense with the flow of the conversation, you can also ask questions throughout.

8. **Follow up:** After the interview, always send a thank-you email to the interviewer. This helps keep you top of mind and shows that you're professional and appreciative of their time.

81. HOW TO WRITE A THANK YOU NOTE AFTER AN INTERVIEW

Sending a thank you note after interviewing is a must. These days, many employers will not hire candidates who do not follow this simple etiquette. According to a recent survey, 75% of hiring managers say they do not receive a thank you note after an interview! [43] Think of the opportunity that provides you to stand out from the crowd.

It can also be strategic by allowing you to remind them of your unique skills and value with personality and professionalism. Follow these steps for success:

1. **Choose the right medium:** Consider whether an email or hand-written note is appropriate, based on the company culture

and your preference. A hand-written note can make a big impact, but it may take longer to arrive.

2. **Personalize it**: Mention specific details from the interview, such as a conversation you had with the interviewer, a project they talked about, or a passion they have for the work that inspires you. This shows that you were engaged in the conversation and are genuinely interested in the company and the role.

3. **Express gratitude:** Thank the interviewer for meeting with you to discuss the role and for considering your candidacy.

4. **Reiterate your interest:** Mention why you're excited about the opportunity and why you'd be a great fit for the role. You can even reiterate some key skills you'll bring to the table if hired.

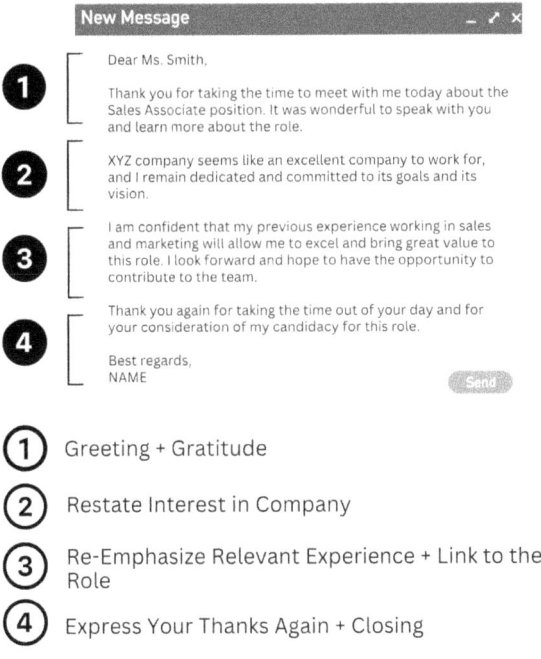

5. **Keep it brief:** Keep the note brief, but don't sacrifice impact. Aim for around 3-4 short paragraphs or just a few sentences each. (It shouldn't read like a school essay).

6. **Proofread:** Before sending, review the note for typos, grammatical errors, and anything else that may give the wrong impression.

7. **Follow up:** Send the thank-you note as soon as possible after the interview, ideally within 24 hours. Never send it more than two days after your interview, or it looks like the interview wasn't a priority in your mind. If you haven't heard back within two weeks or so, it's also appropriate to follow up with a polite email to inquire about the status of your application.

---

82. HOW TO WRITE AN ELEVATOR PITCH

An elevator pitch is a brief, persuasive speech that you can use to spark interest in yourself or an idea. It's called an "elevator pitch" because it should be short enough to deliver during a brief elevator ride. You never know when you may run into a potential job or business opportunity on the spot in your day-to-day life. The idea is that you always have your elevator pitch ready to provide when the opportunity presents itself.

Aim to cover the following points in just 30 seconds to 1 minute:

1. **Start with a hook:** Begin by grabbing the listener's attention with an interesting fact or a question that will pique their interest. You could also explain briefly a mutual connection, where you've seen them before (e.g., at a speaking event), or how you know of their work.

2. **Introduce yourself:** Briefly introduce yourself and provide context about who you are and what you're interested in.

3. **Highlight your strengths:** Identify a few key strengths or experiences that demonstrate why you're the best person for the job or opportunity.

4. **Be specific:** Use specific examples or metrics to support your claims and demonstrate your experience. Anyone can state metrics, but a colorful example drives the point home.

5. **End with a call to action:** Finish your pitch with a call to action, such as requesting a meeting or asking for their contact information.

6. **Practice, practice, practice:** Rehearse your pitch until you can deliver it with ease and confidence. You'll want to sound natural, not robotic or memorized.

① **Introduce Yourself**

"Hi, my name is Eliza. It's great to meet you."

② **Summarize What You Do/ Study**

"I'm a graduating senior from XYZ University majoring in international relations and have strong Spanish speaking skills."

③ **Explain Your Request/ Interest**

"I saw that you have an opening for a Spanish-speaking intern on the migration team, and I wanted to express my strong interest in the position."

④ **Provide a Call-To-Action**

"If you would have an availability, would it be possible to reach out to you with some questions about the role?"

7. **Show your personality:** Don't be afraid to show your personality and let your enthusiasm shine through. People connect with authenticity and energy.

8. **Be prepared to answer questions:** Be ready to answer follow-up questions or provide additional information if asked. Your pitch should spark interest and leave people wanting to know more.

---

83. HOW TO MASTER PROFESSIONAL ETIQUETTE IN THE WORKPLACE

Knowing how to act professionally in the workplace is crucial for making a positive impression on customers, coworkers, and managers - it is a key component of building a successful career that will help you reach your full potential. By mastering workplace etiquette, you'll be able to navigate the professional world with ease and confidence and position yourself for long-term success:

1. **Greet customers and colleagues with eye contact, a smile, and a warm hello:** Saying 'hello' and acknowledging those around you goes further than you think to build a friendly and supportive work environment.

2. **Unplug:** Pulling out your phone to text or surf online may be tempting, but don't do it. Nothing looks more unprofessional, and it also projects a lack of interest in the job, leaving you replaceable.

3. **Keep drama far away:** Don't bring any gossip or drama into the workplace – it makes you the center of attention in a negative way.

4. **Dress appropriately for the workplace:** Make sure your attire is clean, professional, and appropriate. It's always best practice to dress a level up from what you think is expected.

5. **Be punctual:** Arrive on time for meetings and be punctual in returning from breaks. This shows that you respect and value other people's time, and it can help you to maintain a professional image and build trust with your colleagues and superiors.

6. **Practice self-motivation:** Instead of only working when you're told what to do, take the initiative to do what needs to be done. This shows your employer that you are reliable, committed, and capable of going above and beyond to succeed.

7. **Maintain a positive attitude:** Stay optimistic and try to find solutions instead of dwelling on problems. Not only will it help keep you motivated and resilient, even when facing difficult challenges or setbacks, but it will also inspire and uplift those around you.

84. HOW TO WRITE A PROFESSIONAL EMAIL

In today's fast-paced world of technology, email is one of the primary ways we communicate with each other, especially in the workplace. Whether you're sending an inquiry to a potential employer, communicating with a colleague, or following up with a client, it's important to have strong email skills. A poorly written email can damage your credibility, create misunderstandings, and make you appear unprofessional.

Follow these steps to showcase your professionalism and get your message across effectively and efficiently:

1. **Address the recipient correctly:** Start with a proper salutation: 'Dear (name)' is formal and respectful, while 'Hi (name)' or 'Hello (name)' is a bit more casual. Follow formal salutations

using their full name or appropriate title (Mr./Ms./Dr. etc.) if known.

2. Have a clear subject line: Summarize the main point of the email in a concise and specific subject line. This should be a few clear words that tell the receiver almost exactly what to expect when opening the email.

3. Keep it concise: Get straight to the point and avoid long, rambling sentences and excessive use of flowery language. The idea of an email is to make it as easy to read as possible, with short paragraphs of only 1-2 sentences so that the eye can quickly scan over and get the main takeaway.

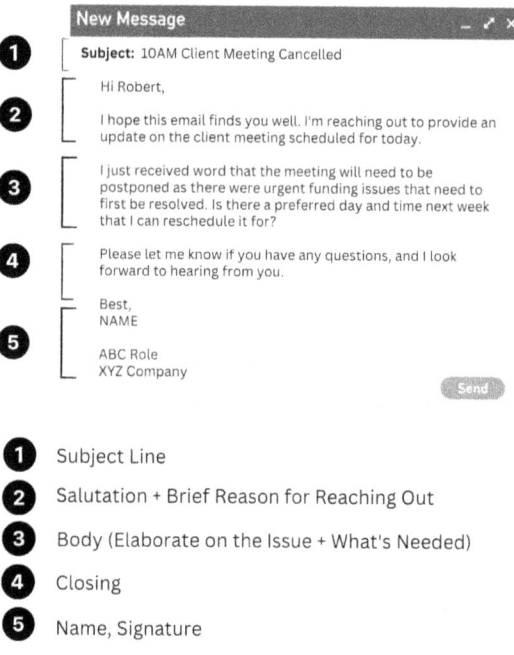

4. Proofread: Read over the email multiple times to catch any errors or typos. Nothing looks more unprofessional than spelling or grammar errors in the workplace.

5. **Use a professional tone:** Avoid using slang, emojis, or overly casual language, even with colleagues you're friends with.

6. **Properly sign-off:** Close the email with a polite and professional closing, such as 'Best regards' or 'Sincerely.'

7. **Re-read before sending:** Always do at least one more careful read-through to ensure your message is clear, there are no spelling errors, and it conveys a positive tone. A pro tip is to add the recipient once your email is fully drafted, so you never accidentally hit 'send' on an unfinished email.

8. **Keep your cool:** Never send an email when angry or upset. It's guaranteed that you will regret it 100% of the time, even if you don't think you will in the moment. Wait until you can think clearly before you decide what action to take (if any).

---

85. HOW TO LEAVE A JOB

Leaving a job can be nerve-wracking, but you can make the transition as smooth as possible with thoughtful planning and preparation. Here are some key steps to help you leave your job on a positive note:

1. **Give sufficient notice:** It's important to give your employer as much notice as possible before you leave your job. This will allow them time to find a replacement and make the transition smoother for everyone involved. A common rule of thumb is to give at least two weeks' notice. As you will want to draw on your boss or mentors for references in the future, and possibly even come back if you're looking for work, you never want to burn bridges. Plus, you never know who they'll know – they could be the reason why you don't get your next job.

2. **Express gratitude:** Before leaving your job, take the time to express gratitude to your employer and coworkers. Even if

things weren't always great, it's the right thing to do and shows professionalism and maturity. Let them know how much you appreciated the opportunity to work with them and the skills you learned on the job.

3. **Discuss your departure with your manager:** Schedule a private meeting with your manager to discuss your departure. This is your chance to explain why you're leaving and how you think the transition could be made easier for everyone involved. Pro tip: keep all emotions and sensitivities out of your reasoning for leaving as much as possible. Stick to the facts, such as looking for something more aligned with skills you want to grow, or with your desired career path, or simply that it provides the flexibility you need for family life, school, etc.

4. **Complete your final tasks:** Before leaving, ensure all your responsibilities have been taken care of and that you've tied up any loose ends. Don't leave your coworkers and boss with a sour taste in their mouths because you dumped all your work onto others.

5. **Return company property:** Return any company property, such as keys, uniforms, and tools you may have been provided.

6. **Stay in touch:** If you want to keep the door open for future opportunities, stay in touch with your employer and coworkers. You will want to use them as a reference in your next role, or who knows, maybe you'll even want to return at some point.

Remember, how you leave your job can have a big impact on your future job prospects, so take the time to do it right.

PART ELEVEN
SOCIAL SAVVY: UNPACKING THE UNWRITTEN RULES OF SOCIAL INTERACTION AND BUILDING HEALTHY BONDS

86. HOW TO TALK TO ANYONE, ANYWHERE

TALKING TO PEOPLE, especially strangers, can be intimidating. But knowing how to small talk can open doors to new connections and opportunities - it's like having a secret superpower to make any social situation a little less awkward and a lot more fun.

1. **Project confidence, and you will feel confident:** Small talk can feel weird and uncomfortable, but it doesn't have to be. Remember that everyone feels awkward when they're making small talk, so you're not alone. Just relax and go with the flow.

2. **Use your surroundings:** This is the perfect strategy for breaking the ice. Anyone can talk about the beautiful or horrible weather happening today, the cool new venue you're in, or their experiences attending this event in the past…the possibilities are endless. Simply look around and make a link to what strikes you.

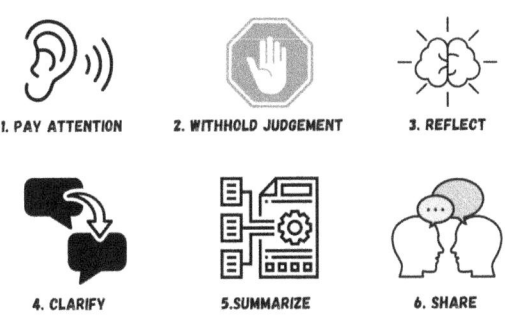

3. **Use reflective listening:** Nerves when socializing with new people can make us want to blurt out anything and everything that comes to our minds, but it makes for better conversation to pause, be present in the moment, and tune into the other person. Comfortable silences are perfectly natural and lead to more

rewarding conversations, as this means intention and thought are being put into what's said.

4. **Ask open-ended questions:** Keep the conversation going with a question asked in a way that would need elaboration to answer rather than a simple 'yes' or 'no.' For example, if you're at a networking event, instead of saying, "Did you like the speaker?" try, "What did you think of that speaker?" Pro tip: add your perspective, like in the following: "What did you think of that speaker? I couldn't believe his story about quitting his job as a famous lawyer to become a motivational speaker instead." This gives more substance for the person to go off of in their response.

5. **Focus on the positive:** Stay away from controversial topics with people you don't know well, and keep things upbeat and with an optimistic tone whenever possible – if not, you risk it taking a sharp turn into awkward.

6. **Don't be afraid to show your true personality:** Have a sense of humor, keep the mood light, be personable and open to who you're talking to, and they will pick up on it.

7. **Know when and how to end the conversation**: There's nothing worse than feeling trapped in a boring conversation or with someone you're just not vibing with. If you're starting to feel like the conversation is going nowhere, it's okay to politely end it and move on. You can say something like, "It was lovely chatting with you; I'm going to go explore a bit; see you around!" and move on to a new person, group, or room wherever you are!

87. HOW TO CARRY A CONVERSATION

Beyond simply striking up small talk with a stranger, it's a separate skill to know how to keep a conversation going. Say you're on a first date or at a work event with colleagues; you'll want to have some conversational strategies up your sleeve. Use the following tips to keep the convo going while making it fun:

1. **Ask questions related to numbers:** Asking questions shows that you are interested and actively listening. It's a seamless way to keep the flow of the conversation going, but the trick lies in not having the other person feel interrogated. Use the strategy of asking questions related to numbers to get the conversation going, such as "How many times have you been here?", "How long ago did that happen?" or "When is it, and what's the schedule like?" These are easy responses for the other person to come up with as you both get into the flow of the conversation.

2. **Use the FORD method:** FORD stands for Family, Occupation, Recreation, and Dreams - it provides a nice balance between easy to talk about and potential for diving deeper (depending on both people's comfort level and willingness to take it there). If you've broken through small talk and hit a lull, ask a question or say something related to one of these topics to get it going again.

3. **Tell a story:** Everyone loves hearing a good story - whether it was something funny that happened to you, something wild and unexpected, or just something weird and fascinating, people love a captivating story that brings them into the experience of another person. It's great to draw upon this method if your conversational partner seems quiet or shy, as it tends to be a deep icebreaker. And you don't have to be an expert storyteller - simply reflect on what types of stories or anecdotes you've repeatedly told people, whether about yourself or something else, and ones that others have been engaged in hearing.

4. **Find common ground:** By exploring shared interests, hobbies, or experiences, you create an immediate sense of connection and foster a deeper understanding of the other person, leading to a more enriching and fruitful conversation.

5. **Go a level deeper:** Once you and your conversation partner have built a bit of a flow in conversation and engaged in a bit of

small talk to break the ice, go a level deeper. You can ask "why?" sorts of questions (but remember to phrase it so that it doesn't sound like an interrogation), or you can share something a level about yourself, encouraging them to follow suit. For example, if they say they play football, you can ask, "Why did you choose football over other sports; what is it specifically about football that you like?" or you could say, "I love football too; some of my favorite memories as a child were going to watch matches every Sunday. What's your favorite team?"

6. **Build upon 'sparks':** Look for glistening sparks in the eyes, raised eyebrows, or excited sparks in their voice to know that you've hit a topic or said something that excited them or deeply piqued their curiosity. Expert conversationalists are always on the lookout for these cues and are ready to dive deeper once they find them.

7. **Ask for advice or recommendations:** If none of the above are working, and you're unsure how to keep the conversation moving, a go-to method is to ask for advice or recommendations related to the event you're at or something you've talked about. You can also switch up topics entirely and ask about recommended movies, books, TV shows, or podcasts.

8. **Treat the conversation like a dance:** Remember that good conversation is just like a dance - both people take turns leading and following, opening first with vulnerability and then stepping back. This is where the magical flow gets created and where true connection and intimacy can flourish!

Being able to carry a conversation beyond small talk can make a big impact on how people perceive you, and it helps you stand out. So master the art of conversation, and you'll have a social superpower under your belt.

88. HOW TO BE A GREAT FRIEND

A good friend is a piece of golden armor; they'll help you weather tough times and celebrate big wins. One of the biggest life lessons to learn is that having good friends by your side makes the joyful times more radiant and the tough times not so bad. So how to have good friends in life? Ultimately, the way to create strong friendships is to be a good friend. Embody the following traits, and your friendships will be made of steel:

1. **Be loyal:** Keep their secrets safe, respect their privacy, and uphold your word when you promise or agree to something. Loyalty creates a bond that stands the test of time, offers security even in the toughest situations, and shows your friend they can count on you.

2. **Be non-judgmental:** Respect and appreciate your differences – in interests, background, or how you see life. If everyone was exactly the same, life would be pretty boring. When we can be ourselves without fear of being judged, we can open up, grow, and support each other in meaningful ways.

3. **Make time for one another:** In a world of constant distractions, a great friend knows that making time for one another is the ultimate sign of love and respect. Whether it's a phone call, a text, or a coffee date, taking the time to show up for one another creates a sense of closeness like none other.

4. **Support each other in wins and challenges:** A great friend is always there to cheer you on during your victories and lend a helping hand when things get tough. A supportive friendship creates a safe environment for ongoing growth and development.

5. **Be vulnerable:** Great friends are not afraid to be vulnerable with one another, as it helps to build trust and emotional intimacy. Being open about your feelings and experiences can

deepen your connection and create a level of authenticity you didn't know was possible.

6. **Apologize when you've made a mistake:** A key trait of a great friend is the ability to recognize when you've done something wrong, take responsibility for your actions, and apologize. Being able to apologize with sincerity and humility shows that you value the relationship and want to make things right, leaving the bond even stronger than it was before.

What else would you add to this list? There's no one else like you on this earth, which means you have some awesome and unique strengths as a friend. Tune into what those are, and don't be afraid to ramp them up a notch!

89. HOW TO KEEP YOUR WORD

As the saying goes, "you're only as good as your word." Words are the way we communicate and connect with other humans on this earth, and if our word can't be trusted, or we can't trust others' words, life becomes a whole lot more chaotic.

Having to break your promises every once in a while is understandable; we're only human, after all. Say you promised to attend a social gathering, but you're behind on studying for an exam and need to stay in to feel confident the next day. There's a difference between breaking your word simply because what you agreed to is now inconvenient to you or because you no longer want to do it, versus having other priorities come up in your life that you have to attend to.

Earning people's trust may be one of the most difficult things on this planet, which is why keeping your word is so valuable – in the workplace, to friends, family, loved ones, and to anyone.

Keeping our word is also not just about being respected by others but also about us respecting ourselves. If we make a promise to others or ourselves and then make up an excuse not to keep it, we're training our brain that our word is optional and not to be taken seriously.

Here's what you can do to always keep your word:

1. **Think carefully before agreeing to something:** It's best practice not to agree immediately. You can say something like, "that sounds fun; let me make sure I'll be able to come, and then I'll get back to you."

2. **When you do make a commitment, write it down:** Not only does this help you remember and solidify your plans for yourself, but you can also make it a habit of why you want to do that thing so that you remember the excitement or other positive emotions that led you to accept it in the first place. If it's a professional or academic commitment, make a note of how it will contribute to your growth.

3. **Think of commitments in the future as if happening in the now:** Often, we easily agree to things in the future because they feel so distant and as if they may not actually occur. Then once it's time to do them, we realize it never aligned with our interests or values. So before agreeing to things, ask yourself, "would I actually want to do this if it was about to happen right now?"

4. **View your commitments as a privilege:** Shift your perspectives to view honoring your commitments as a way to show the people in your life that you respect and care about them. If you expect them to show up for you, you need to do the same for them.

90. HOW TO APOLOGIZE

Apologies are not just about saying sorry but are also about harnessing the power to restore and rebuild relationships. By knowing how to craft a meaningful apology that addresses hurt feelings, we cultivate one of life's most important skills–solving conflict with compassion while strengthening our connections. Because ultimately, without relationships, life would be pretty lonely.

1. **Own your mistake:** If you don't feel like you did anything wrong, perhaps it's not the best time to force an ingenuine apology. Instead, take time to reflect on why the other person is hurt. If you're unsure why the other person is upset, you can try something like, "You seem upset with me. Did I do something wrong?"

2. **Accept that it's not about being right:** No one can deny there are multiple sides to every story – there is never a right and a wrong. Accept this and remember the bigger picture here is to maintain and strengthen a relationship that is important to you. This means that the outcome of the conversation should not be centered in any way around who was right and who was wrong. Instead, acknowledge the hurt they are feeling.

3. **Avoid "you" statements:** This puts the blame on the other person when what's needed is a focus on you taking accountability for your role in what happened. You can use "I" statements to do this, as well as to explain your own feelings. But remember, there should be no blame or deflecting of responsibility, simply a sharing of how you felt in the situation and how you feel now.

4. **Come to a resolution:** A best practice for doing this is to ask for forgiveness, describe what you learned and how or why you won't do the same thing or in the same way in the future, and show empathy for the other person's experience. This will let you both find peace and move on together stronger.

How To Say a Genuine Apology

1 Say what you're apologizing for:
"I'm sorry for..."

2 State why you were in the wrong:
"It was wrong of me because..."

3 Accept full responsibility for what happened:
"I take full accountability of what I said/did..."

4 Ask how you can make things right:
"What can I do to make things better?"

5 Commit to learning from what happened:
"Moving forward, I promise to..."

6 Request their forgiveness:
"Will you accept my apology?"

These are not genuine apologies:

"I'm sorry but..."   "I'm sorry you feel that way..."
"You misunderstood what I meant"   "What about that time you..."

91. HOW TO FORGIVE

When we experience pain at the hands of someone close to us, it can be hard to forgive. But holding on to grudges and resentment won't lead anywhere good - don't let them stand in the way of finding your own peace.

It shows maturity and wisdom to understand that everyone makes mistakes. Often those we love don't intend to hurt us, but they are simply doing the best with the information and skills that they had at the time.

1. **Address your inner pain:** Feel your emotions – embrace the anger, sadness, or feelings of betrayal. Emotions are real, and you have a right to feel how you feel. If you need to scream into

a pillow, go for it. Understanding your emotions, why you feel that way, and releasing them (in a healthy way) allows them to move through your body so that they can be completely let go.

2. **Reflect on the situation:** Once you're ready, try to switch perspectives and see the situation from all sides. Can you find any insight into why the other person may have acted the way they did? It doesn't mean it was right or that it wasn't hurtful, but it allows us to understand other people's humanity and complexity.

3. **Make the decision to forgive:** But only do so when you're ready. Once you've done the steps above and are ready to make peace with the situation, resolve to let go of negative emotions like anger and resentment, allowing space for other good things to enter your life.

HOW CAN I KNOW IF I'M READY TO FORGIVE?

1 Is there something I'm still holding onto in this situation, or can I fully let go?

2 Can I move on without holding resentment towards this person?

3 Can I see their humanity in this situation, even if I don't agree with what happened, or if what they did was wrong?

Remember that forgiveness does not necessarily mean you have to have a conversation with another person or let them back into your life. Learning to forgive is ultimately about freeing yourself of internal pain rather than holding onto it and giving your power away. As Nelson Mandela said, "Resentment is like drinking poison and hoping it will kill your enemies." Choose to live in peace and forgive instead.

---

92. HOW TO STOP BULLYING WHEN YOU SEE IT IN PERSON

By taking action and standing up against bullying when you see it, you have the power to not only make the world a better place, but also show your courage, kindness, and leadership skills, all while being a protector for someone in need! And that's not just an exaggeration – standing up for someone being bullied can save a life.

Here's what to do if you see someone being bullied in person:

1. **Question the bullying behavior:** Redirect the conversation or address the behavior directly to help shift the focus and stop the bullying. Speaking up and telling the bully to stop is also an assertive option.

2. **Use humor to say something funny and redirect the conversation:** This diffuses the situation by lightening the energy so that the bully moves on. However, sometimes laughter can egg the bully on, so use your judgment in telling them directly to stop what they're doing versus making a light joke to break things up.

3. **Draw upon strength in numbers:** Bullies typically target people when they're alone and isolated. Speak up and intervene as a group, even just as two people, to show that several people don't agree with the bullying. You can also simply walk up to the situation and use your presence as a way to diffuse the situation.

4. **Walk with the person who is the target of bullying:** This removes the individual from potential bullying interactions while showing your support. The presence of another does wonders.

5. **Show your support:** Reach out privately to check in with the person who was bullied to let them know you do not agree with it and that you care about them and how they're feeling. Even what may seem like a small action to you can make all the difference.

Remember to be an upstander, not a bystander: you are a leader and compassionate human, not someone who stays silent to injustice and cruelty in the world. As the saying goes, "Be the change you wish to see in the world."

93. HOW TO IDENTIFY WHAT TYPE OF RELATIONSHIP YOU'D LIKE TO CREATE

Before getting into any relationship, it's essential to understand your values, needs, and long-term vision for your life. This will increase your chances of finding happiness and help you avoid heartache and disappointment, especially when you notice misalignments from the outset.

By taking the time to reflect on what values are most important to you and what kind of relationship you'd like to create with your partner, you can make sure that the relationship is built on a solid foundation conducive to long-term success. How would your dream relationship feel? What kinds of things would you do together and for one another?

Knowing what qualities or characteristics define a successful partnership for you will help you to be able to spot which connections have potential worth exploring early on, while also signaling which aren't aligned with your ideal vision, just like a roadmap guiding you:

1. **Get to know yourself first:** Knowing yourself is the foundation for any healthy relationship. Taking the time to understand your own values, needs, and boundaries for well-being allows you to stay true to yourself and show up as the authentic person you are, so that you can create genuine connections with others while also knowing when to walk away.

2. **Ask yourself why you want a relationship:** Are you looking for a relationship that provides emotional support and intimacy? Do you want one that allows for growth and adventure? Remember that at the core, relationships are a place to give and support another person, not to be a taker. When both are givers, that's where the magic happens.

3. **Determine your non-negotiables:** Take some time to reflect on what you need and want in a relationship. Consider the qualities and values important to you, such as trust, communication, and mutual respect. How does this need to show up for you to feel safe and seen in a relationship? Remember that humans are complex, and they need to be taught how to love us in the way that we need to feel loved. So instead of jumping to conclusions if someone isn't doing what you expect, have an open conversation about it instead.

4. **Determine your dealbreakers:** Often, the opposite of a non-negotiable is a dealbreaker. What sorts of things can you absolutely not have in a partnership – maybe it's a trait, such as smoking, or perhaps it's a long-term vision that differs, such as you want to move across the country, while they never want to move away from their hometown. A dealbreaker could also be something related to a relationship dynamic, such as someone who doesn't communicate regularly even after you've respectfully expressed your needs and what that looks like to you.

5. **Become the qualities on your list:** You can't expect someone else to embody your desired traits and characteristics if you don't do them yourself. This is the secret key many people miss –become the traits you desire in an ideal relationship.

6. **Be open to things you weren't expecting:** Don't cut off the potential for something great just because it doesn't show up as you initially expected – be open to surprises, and you never know what life will bring your way.

---

94. HOW TO DATE

If you're a teenager navigating the dating world, it can feel overwhelming and like you're in uncharted territory. It's normal to be nervous or unsure of what to do when figuring out how to date. It doesn't have to be intimidating, though! By following a few simple guidelines, you'll be able to understand more about yourself and be more confident when it comes to dating.

Here are some tips that can help:

1. **Take the time to get to know yourself first:** Understanding who you are - your values, likes, and dislikes - will make it easier for you to know what kind of person you want in a partner. Spend time doing activities that help you learn about yourself and not just focus on relationships with others.

2. **Enjoy the journey:** Don't put too much pressure on yourself or others. One of the benefits of dating is getting an opportunity to meet new people, so make sure to try meeting different types of people rather than limiting yourself from the start.

3. **Be honest with your intentions:** If you're looking for something casual, let your date know upfront. Communication is key in any relationship, and it's important that both parties are

honest with each other about their expectations so that there aren't any surprises down the road.

4. **Make sure that both parties feel comfortable during dates:** Everyone has their own pace when it comes to intimacy, whether physical or emotional, so make sure that both people feel respected and safe throughout those steps, if they choose them at all.

5. **Have fun:** Dating should be enjoyable - don't take things too seriously. Keep safety a priority, and remember not to rush into anything before you feel ready! Listen to your gut, but learn to tell the difference between intuition and fear.

SELF-REFLECTIVE QUESTIONS IN DATING & RELATIONSHIPS

1 Are we a good team fit?

2 Do our personalities naturally mesh well or clash?

3 Do we have a similar life vision and goals?

4 Do I accept and appreciate them for who they are now, rather than their potential or who I want them to be?

95. HOW TO STRENGTHEN ANY RELATIONSHIP

Having strong relationships is an important aspect of a fulfilling life. Whether it's with family, friends, or romantic partners, having a support system and feeling connected to others can bring joy, comfort, and security. But how do you make sure your relationships are as strong as possible? Here are some tips to help you strengthen any relationship, not just a romantic one:

1. **Communicate openly:** Open and effective communication is the key to any healthy relationship. Listen actively, be honest, and express your feelings clearly and respectfully. Our minds can't be read, so respectful communication is the foundation for all connections.

2. **Show appreciation:** Expressing gratitude and acknowledging what your loved ones do for you can go a long way. Instead of focusing on what isn't perfect, we can choose to focus on all of the good things they do for us and those they care about.

3. **Spend quality time:** Make an effort to spend quality time together, whether through shared interests or simply spending time together doing something you both enjoy. This means being fully present – connected with body language (eye contact, body posture) and your phone put away!

4. **Compromise:** In any relationship, it's essential to be willing to compromise and work together to find solutions that benefit both parties. Relationships are not a place to keep score but where both people go to give – there is almost always a middle ground that works for all involved.

5. **Be supportive:** When someone you care about is going through a tough time, be there for them with love, understanding, and support. Simply showing up with an open heart and no judgment can completely change someone's outlook on life and the challenge they're going through.

Strengthening relationships takes effort and dedication, but the reward is worth it. By putting in the work, you can build stronger, more fulfilling connections with the people you care about. Relationships are what makes us human, after all, and a life without relationships would be dull indeed.

PART TWELVE
DIGITAL DEFENSE: MASTERING ESSENTIAL SKILLS FOR KEEPING YOURSELF SAFE IN THE WILD WILD WEB

96. HOW TO PROTECT YOUR DIGITAL FOOTPRINT

A DIGITAL FOOTPRINT is like a trail you leave behind wherever you go online. Just like how you can see footprints in the sand, others can see your online actions and information.

According to a recent study, 70% of employers say that they screen potential employees on social media and that what they find impacts whether or not they decide to hire that person. And from that same study, 51% of employers found social media content that caused them to pass on an otherwise good candidate. Some of these reasons included provocative or inappropriate photos or information (46%), bad-mouthing a previous company or fellow employees (36%), and poor communication skills (32%). Another survey found that 40% of college admissions officers visited applicants' social media pages when making decisions.[44]

It can't be overstated how important it is to keep your digital footprint clean and controlled. Otherwise, unintended consequences may arise, such as reputation damage, lost job or college opportunities, cyberbullying from being made a target, or even legal consequences.

So what can you do to protect your footprint? It's easier than you may think:

1. **Make sure you're on private**: Make sure your profile and posts are limited to your family and friends and not open to the public.

2. **Be careful of what sites you visit:** This is traceable, so don't visit anything you wouldn't want others to know about. Insecure sites also pose a security risk in terms of viruses and scams.

3. **Think before you post:** Even if you have privacy settings turned on, what goes on the internet stays on the internet, and there will always be a record of it. It's especially important to think about how any words or images you use could potentially harm another person, like a meme meant as a joke that could harm your reputation down the line.

4. **Search yourself:** Do a quick Google search of your name to see what comes up – if you wouldn't be proud of your grandmother seeing it, clean it up! Make sure to review this periodically, and especially before submitting school or job applications.

97. HOW TO AVOID PHISHING AND OTHER SCAMS

Do you ever get suspicious emails, voicemails, or texts that seem too good to be true? Or what about offers for free products or services, or notifications from your bank or utility provider asking you to enter your login credentials? In today's fast-moving world of technological innovation, it's absolutely essential to master the ropes of recognizing phishing and other online scams.

Phishing is an online scam where scammers pose as someone else to trick you into giving them personal information like your bank account number, credit card number, or Social Security number. They might do this by sending you an email that looks like it's from a company  you know, by creating a fake website that looks like a real website, or by leaving you a voicemail with a number to call back. Here's how you can spot phishing and scam attempts:

1. **Don't enter personal information on websites unless you're sure they're legitimate:** When shopping online or doing your banking, make sure you're on a legitimate website before entering any personal information. Secure websites have URLs that start with "https://" and have a lock icon next to them. Also, be careful on open Wi-fi networks, as the public network means anyone could see confidential information you provide while connected.

2. **Be suspicious of unsolicited emails:** Whenever you receive an email from someone you don't know or from a company you do know but didn't expect to hear from, your internal alarm bells should always go off. Never click on any links in an unknown email, and don't reply. If you're unsure if the email is real, contact the company directly to find out.

3. **Be cautious of urgency:** If you sense urgency and don't know the sender, it's likely a scam attempt. Real emails from legitimate sources are unlikely to ask for urgent or immediate actions, such as clicking on a link, providing sensitive information, or downloading an attachment. Before taking any action, take a moment to confirm the source of the email and whether it is actually sending you information you requested.

4. **Be careful about any job offers that you receive online:** Did you apply for a job or contact anyone for a job? If you didn't, the content is suspicious and could be a scammer posing as a recruiter. Do some research about the company or business, and proceed with caution.

5. **Know who to contact if you think you've been scammed:** If you think you may have given personal information to a scammer, contact your bank or credit card company right away to inform them of any accounts that may have been compromised.

98. HOW TO PROTECT YOURSELF FROM BEING HACKED

As a generation of digital natives, you and your peers are more exposed to potential cyber security threats than ever before. Plenty of hackers out there would love to get their hands on all sorts of personal information about you, and they are looking for one little slip-up in online privacy or security to make their move.

Follow these tips to ensure your personal and financial data is kept safe:

Strong Passwords **Are**:

 12-15 characters: longer is better

 A random mix of letters, numbers, symbols, & capitalization

 Unique to each site, never repeated anywhere

Strong Passwords **Don't** Do This:

 Use any real words that could be found in a dictionary

 Use any personal information like pet names, birthdays, or addresses

☒ Use any consecutive series like 123 or ABC

1. **Use strong passwords and never share them with anyone:** A strong password should be at least twelve characters long and contain a mix of random uppercase and lowercase letters, numbers, and symbols. Avoid using easily guessed words like "password" or "123456", and never use the same password for multiple accounts. It's better to memorize your passwords or keep them in a secure location than to use autofill, which, if

hacked, can easily provide a hacker access to multiple accounts.

2. **Keep your profile secure:** Choose who can see your posts, friends list, and profile information. Only share necessary personal information, such as your name and profile picture.

3. **Keep your computer security up-to-date, including antivirus and anti-malware programs:** Old vulnerabilities are being exploited by hackers who discover vulnerabilities. Keeping software up-to-date will help protect your computer from being infected with viruses or malware that scammers can use to get your personal information. You can set your software to update automatically, or you can check for updates manually on a regular basis.

4. **Use a firewall:** A firewall is a piece of software that helps to protect your computer from unauthorized access. A firewall can be used to block incoming attacks from known hackers as well as outgoing connections to malicious websites. Most routers have a built-in firewall, but you can install a firewall program on your computer for additional protection.

5. **Be careful when downloading apps, and make sure they are reputable:** Hackers often embed malicious code into files they host on their websites or share through email attachments. If you download one of these files and open it, the code will execute and allow the hacker to gain access to your system. Only download files from known and secure sources, and be sure to scan all files with antivirus software before opening them.

99. HOW TO DEAL WITH CYBERBULLYING

Recent research shows that a whopping 37% of teens have been bullied online, while 30% say it's happened more than once.[45] Cyberbullying takes a major toll on mental health and well-being, and, unfortunately, it's most likely here to stay as long as social media is around.

1. **Don't respond:** Avoid engaging with the bully, as this could escalate the situation and give them more ammunition.

2. **Block and report:** Block the bully on social media, and report any abusive behavior to the platform's moderators.

3. **Save evidence:** Keep screenshots or saved copies of any messages, posts, or comments that are harmful.

4. **Talk to a trusted adult:** Share your experience with a parent, teacher, or another trusted adult who can support you and help you find a solution.

5. **Avoid negative online spaces:** Limit your exposure to negative comments and cyberbullying by avoiding certain social media groups or online communities.

6. **Focus on self-care:** Take care of your emotional well-being by doing things you enjoy, being kind to yourself, and reaching out to friends or a counselor if needed.

7. **If witnessing someone else being cyberbullied**: Don't engage with the cyberbully online; simply report the incident to the platform's administrators. Support the victim by reaching out and offering help or resources, and encourage the victim to block and report the cyberbully.

Remember, cyberbullying is not your fault, and you don't have to deal with it alone. Never take a cyberbully's words personally - when someone is nasty and hurtful online, it's most often the case that they're feeling unhappy or frustrated with their own life. They take it out on others in a cowardly way by hiding behind a screen instead of confronting people face-to-face. So remember who you are; imagine having a barrier of titanium for an energy shield, and let it all roll right off you!

100. HOW TO STAY SAFE ON SOCIAL MEDIA

Social media has immense potential for connection, self-expression, and entertainment. However, this vast power also brings significant risks and potential harm if not utilized appropriately.

Imagine the entire population of the world (8 billion, by the way).[46] Now imagine more than half of them are active social media users! It's true - 4.8 billion people are snapping, posting, and sharing on social media every day, and this number is only growing.[47] So whether  you love or hate it, social media is here to stay, and it's critical to know how to use it safely.

1. **Respect others' opinions, even if you have differing views:** Social media has become a place where people feel comfortable tearing each other down because they are comfortable hiding behind a screen – let's all vow to contribute more positivity to the world instead.

2. **Never meet up with strangers:** Be cautious of online strangers and never meet them in person. It's all too easy for people to fake a profile and act on ill intent.

3. **Don't believe everything you see online:** Verify information before sharing it.

4. **Assess how you feel:** Limit the amount of time you spend on social media and take breaks if you feel overwhelmed.

5. **Adjust your settings:** Check your privacy settings within each social media platform and adjust them to your preferences. For

example, it's in your best interest to allow restrictions to messaging so that only people you know can contact you and that your geolocation is turned off when your share photos or make posts.

6. **If something doesn't feel right, trust your instincts:** Sharing any concerns or hesitations with a trusted adult is crucial, as your safety should always come first. Remember, it's always better to be safe than sorry, especially if you're worried or have experienced something troubling online. Seek their advice promptly and take the necessary actions to protect yourself.

PART THIRTEEN
THE FINAL LESSON: THINGS YOU SHOULD KNOW THAT WE CAN'T TEACH YOU

101. THINGS YOU SHOULD KNOW THAT WE CAN'T TEACH YOU

1. A joke that gets you every time
2. How to see the best in others
3. A dream that drives you forward
4. How to rock your favorite outfit for confidence
5. What lights you up inside
6. How to cheer yourself up on a gloomy day
7. The joy of creating something from scratch with your own hands
8. The feeling of complete immersion into another universe through the power of a good book
9. How to enjoy spending time with yourself
10. The feeling of discovering music that speaks to your soul
11. How to embrace change as the only constant in life
12. The joy of dancing like no one's watching
13. The joy of experiencing new culture and cuisines through travel and exploration
14. The ability to adapt to new situations and think on your feet
15. The satisfaction of completing a challenging workout
16. The beauty of experiencing nature and the outdoors in a new way
17. The feeling of peace after an extended break and unplugging from technology
18. Finding your voice and speaking up for what you believe in
19. The sense of connection that comes from giving back in service
20. The realization that life is a journey, not a destination

THE FUTURE IS YOURS

THE LIFE SKILLS you've gained in this book are just as crucial as academic skills. The ability to budget, network, communicate effectively, and prioritize are the foundational skills that will empower you to navigate life's complexities with confidence and ease. By mastering these skills, you'll be equipped to build a future that aligns with your aspirations and fills you with happiness and fulfillment.

Now that you have all the tools, it's time to take action. Small steps, such as understanding your spending, strengthening the relationships in your life, putting your physical and mental health first, and developing daily habits that support your goals, can put you light years ahead of your peers on a pathway to success. You have the ultimate resource on your side that no one can get more of, no matter how much money or status they have – and that is time.

Remember that success is not about perfection but progress. Keep learning, growing, and improving, and you'll be amazed at what you can achieve.

As we conclude this journey towards a better, more fulfilling life, I wish you all the best in applying these skills and creating a bright future for yourself. Embrace the challenges, take action, and create a life you love!

PAY IT FORWARD

If you learned something new in this book that you believe will help you to better your life, please consider leaving a review on your platform of purchase to help other teenagers find it.

You can do so in one of three ways:

1. By following this URL: https://www.amazon.com/review/create-review/?asin=B0C1DRYV17

2. By scanning the QR code below with your mobile device:

3. You can also find the listing on Amazon in your Orders page and click 'Write a Customer Review.'

Your review will help others to find this book and guide other teenagers in your shoes towards the same life-changing insights you've gained. Thank you for taking the time to pay it forward!

A GIFT TO OUR READERS

AS A THANK YOU FOR INVESTING IN THIS BOOK, WE'D LIKE TO GIFT:

https://teeninsights.activehosted.com/f/5

Free Bonus #1: The Life Skills Mastery Toolbox ($22 value)

A 35-page workbook of fillable and printable activity sheets to put the skills learned in this book to practice, to:

- Design a life vision, including purpose, profession, finances, and relationships
- Implement evidence-based tools for emotional regulation and self-care
- Create and integrate daily, weekly, and monthly routines balancing productivity & well-being
- Set SMART goals and create action plans to build the life you want

Free Bonus #2: Teen Empowerment & Self-Reliance Series Book #2 ($16 value)

Plus a free copy of our next book in the teen and young adult empowerment and self-reliance series.

Scan the QR code with your mobile device to receive your free gifts as a token of our thanks and appreciation:

Or visit https://teeninsights.activehosted.com/f/5

(All of these bonuses are 100% free, no strings attached, with no details required except your email address. Unsubscribe at any time.)

NOTES

10. 69. HOW TO SAVE YOUR HARD-EARNED CASH

1. Note an 8% average annualized return is assumed, which is a conservative estimate for the S&P 500, a top-performing U.S. stock market index fund.

REFERENCES

1. Cfc, A. A. (2022, March 16). *Study: More Than One in Four Americans Say Their Debt is Unmanageable.* OppLoans. https://www.opploans.com/oppu/articles/personal-finance-study-2022/
2. Winters, M. (2022b, April 29). *73% of people don't regularly follow a budget—and that's OK, says a financial therapist.* CNBC. https://www.cnbc.com/2022/04/29/its-ok-to-not-follow-a-budget-says-a-financial-therapist.html
3. Team, S., Team, S., & S. (2023, February 4). *Stress statistics 2023: How common is stress and who's most affected?* The Checkup. https://www.singlecare.com/blog/news/stress-statistics/
4. S. (2018, June 15). *Most Americans have no idea what's going on under the hood.* New York Post. https://nypost.com/2018/06/15/most-americans-have-no-idea-whats-going-on-under-the-hood/
5. D., & D. (2021, October 4). *81% of recent college grads wish they were taught more life skills before graduation.* Digitalhub US. https://swnsdigital.com/us/2021/07/eighty-one-percent-of-recent-college-graduates-wish-they-were-taught-more-life-skills-before-graduating/
6. Reinicke, C. (2022, June 1). *54% of teenagers feel unprepared to finance their futures, survey shows.* cnbc.com. https://www.cnbc.com/2022/06/01/54percent-of-teens-feel-unprepared-to-finance-their-futures-survey-shows.html
7. Solutions, R. (2021, September 24). *The Truth About Teens and Credit Cards.* Ramsey Solutions. https://www.ramseysolutions.com/debt/the-truth-about-teens-and-credit-cards
8. Boeree, C. G. (n.d.). *Socrates, Plato, and Aristotle.* http://webspace.ship.edu/cgboer/athenians.html
9. Marksberry, K. (2022, April 6). *Teens - The American Institute of Stress.* The American Institute of Stress. https://www.stress.org/teens
10. Vargas, R. A. (2023, January 27). World's oldest person on the keys to longevity: 'stay away from toxic people.' The Guardian. https://www.theguardian.com/us-news/2023/jan/26/worlds-oldest-person-115-maria-branyas-morera-california
11. *How Does Food Impact Health? | Taking Charge of Your Health & Wellbeing.* (n.d.). Taking Charge of Your Health & Wellbeing. https://www.takingcharge.csh.umn.edu/how-does-food-impact-health
12. Harvard Health. (2021, November 16). *Foods that fight inflammation.* https://www.health.harvard.edu/staying-healthy/foods-that-fight-inflammation
13. Study shows how serotonin and a popular anti-depressant affect the gut's microbiota. (2019, September 19). ScienceDaily. https://www.sciencedaily.com/releases/2019/09/190906092809.htm

14. Ms, M. a. a. M. (2019, March 13). *Can exercise extend your life?* Harvard Health. https://www.health.harvard.edu/blog/can-exercise-extend-your-life-2019031316207
15. Bains, P. (2020, January 9). Exercise is key to living longer. https://www.allinahealth.org/healthysetgo/move/exercise-is-key-to-living-longer
16. The Mental Health Benefits of Exercise - HelpGuide.org. (n.d.). HelpGuide.org. https://www.helpguide.org/articles/healthy-living/the-mental-health-benefits-of-exercise.htm
17. Cherry, K. (2023, January 23). Effects of Lack of Sleep on Mental Health. Verywell Mind. https://www.verywellmind.com/how-sleep-affects-mental-health-4783067
18. Get Enough Sleep - MyHealthfinder | health.gov. (2021, August 1). https://health.gov/myhealthfinder/healthy-living/mental-health-and-relationships/get-enough-sleep
19. Zhang, X., Liu, Y., Li, S., Lichtenstein, A. H., Chen, S., Na, M., Veldheer, S., Xing, A., Wang, Y., Wu, S., & Gao, X. (2021). Alcohol consumption and risk of cardiovascular disease, cancer and mortality: a prospective cohort study. Nutrition Journal, 20(1). https://doi.org/10.1186/s12937-021-00671-y
20. Rowe, K. (2022, April 12). How to Avoid Harmful Toxins in Your Life | BrainMD. BrainMD Blog. https://brainmd.com/blog/how-to-get-rid-of-harmful-toxins/
21. Know the Risks of E-cigarettes for Young People | Know the Risks: E-cigarettes & Young People | U.S. Surgeon General's Report. (n.d.). Know the Risks: E-Cigarettes and Young People | U.S. Surgeon General's Report. https://e-cigarettes.surgeongeneral.gov/knowtherisks.html
22. 3 ways vaping affects mental health. (2021, September 10). Truth Initiative. https://truthinitiative.org/research-resources/targeted-communities/3-ways-vaping-affects-mental-health
23. House, J. S., Landis, K. R., & Umberson, D. (n.d.). Social Relationships and Health. https://www.science.org/doi/abs/10.1126/science.3399889.
24. Seppala, E. (2022, July 19). Connectedness & Health: The Science of Social Connection - The Center for Compassion and Altruism Research and Education. The Center for Compassion and Altruism Research and Education. http://ccare.stanford.edu/uncategorized/connectedness-health-the-science-of-social-connection-infographic/
25. Novotney, A. (n.d.). The risks of social isolation. https://www.apa.org. https://www.apa.org/monitor/2019/05/ce-corner-isolation
26. Gordon, S. (2022, September 29). Benefits of Mindfulness for Kids and Teens. Verywell Family. https://www.verywellfamily.com/benefits-of-mindfulness-for-kids-4769017
27. Stress effects on the body. (2018, November 1). https://www.apa.org. https://www.apa.org/topics/stress/body
28. What to Know About Mindfulness for Teens. (2021, March 25). WebMD. https://www.webmd.com/balance/what-to-know-about-mindfulness-for-teens

29. Family Resource Sheet #1: Read the Label First - Why the Label Matters. (2015). scholastic.com. https://www.scholastic.com/otcmedsafety/pdfs/family/ResourceSheets_English.pdf#page=4
30. Is it safe to mix acetaminophen and alcohol? (2022, October 6). https://www.medicalnewstoday.com/articles/322813
31. Cold Versus Flu. (2022, September 29). Centers for Disease Control and Prevention. https://www.cdc.gov/flu/symptoms/coldflu.htm
32. Mindbodygreen. (2023, February 3). 2023's Dirty Dozen & Clean 15 Lists Are Out: Here's What To Know. Mindbodygreen. https://www.mindbodygreen.com/articles/ewg-dirty-dozen-and-clean-15-lists
33. Environmental Working Group – Know your choices | Environmental Working Group. (2021, November 3). EWG. https://www.ewg.org/
34. Stearns, S. (2020, January 20). What do labels really mean? Organic, Natural, Cage-Free... Extension News. https://news.extension.uconn.edu/2019/12/09/what-do-labels-really-mean-organic-natural-cage-free/
35. BSc, K. G. (2022, December 20). 9 Health Benefits of Eating Eggs. Healthline. https://www.healthline.com/nutrition/proven-health-benefits-of-eggs
36. Rd, R. R. M. (2018, October 16). Is White Rice Healthy or Bad for You? Healthline. https://www.healthline.com/nutrition/is-white-rice-bad-for-you
37. Carli, K. (2023, January 24). 15 Types Of Rice And How To Perfectly Cook Them. Tasting Table. https://www.tastingtable.com/764585/types-of-rice-and-how-to-perfectly-cook-them/
38. Dahlgreen, W. (2014, August 27). The great sheet washing divide: which group are you in? YouGov. https://yougov.co.uk/topics/politics/articles-reports/2014/08/27/5-weeks-when-unwashed-bedsheets-become-disgusting
39. Fight or Flight. (n.d.). UT Austin. https://fireprevention.utexas.edu/firesafety/fight-or-flight
40. SDG Target 3.6 Road traffic injuries (n.d.). https://www.who.int/data/gho/data/themes/topics/sdg-target-3_6-road-traffic-injuries
41. Road Traffic Injuries and Deaths—A Global Problem. (2023, January 10). Centers for Disease Control and Prevention. https://www.cdc.gov/injury/features/global-road-safety/index.html
42. Ramsey Solutions. (n.d.). Investment Calculator. https://www.ramseysolutions.com/retirement/investment-calculator
43. G., & G. (2018a, January 10). Why You Should 100% Write A Thank You Note After Your Next Job Interview. Girlboss. https://girlboss.com/blogs/read/thank-you-note-job-interview
44. What Every Teen Needs to Know About Their Digital Footprint | Net Nanny. (2023, March 2). (C) 2001-2020 Copyright Content: Content Watch Holdings, Inc. Copyright Design: Content Watch Holdings, Inc. https://www.netnanny.com/blog/what-every-teen-needs-to-know-about-their-digital-footprint/
45. Hershenson, K. (2022, September 14). 9 Ways to Deal with Cyberbullying. Talkspace. https://www.talkspace.com/blog/7-ways-to-deal-with-cyberbullying/

46. World Population Clock: 8 Billion People (LIVE, 2023) - Worldometer. (n.d.). https://www.worldometers.info/world-population/
47. Global Social Media Statistics — DataReportal – Global Digital Insights. (n.d.). DataReportal – Global Digital Insights. https://datareportal.com/social-media-users